THE COMPLETE GUIDE TO
DELAWARE
HISTORIC MARKERS

Written by
JOE A. SWISHER

Photography by
ROGER MILLER

ROGER MILLER IN HIS STUDIO

JOE SWISHER

image publishing, ltd.

1411 Hollins Street / Union Square
Baltimore, MD 21223-2417
TEL 410-566-1222   FAX 410-233-1241
WEB PAGE rogermillerphoto.com
EMAIL rmpl.ipl@verizon.net

DEDICATION

I would like to dedicate this book to my wife and friend, Sue.
Joe A. Swisher, Author, 10-01-2001

I would like to dedicate this book to Ruth Dora Miller, my mom, who gave me life, made me strong and always encouraged me to explore new places.
Roger Miller, Photographer, 10-01-2001

SPECIAL THANKS

A very special thanks to **EVERYONE IN DELAWARE** who created and preserved all the wondrous historic sites over the years which we visited and photographed, as well as all those that we did not get to. Without your efforts this book would not have been possible. A very special thanks to everyone who assisted me in getting access to the sites and permission to do photos. A very special thanks to **RUSS McCABE**, of the Delaware Public Archives for his support, assistance and advice in this book's development and publication. A very special thanks to **GOVERNOR RUTH ANN MINNER** for allowing us to meet and photograph her and for doing the foreword to this book. A very special thanks to **REPRESENTATIVE WAYNE SMITH** for his vision and support in doing this book and other important projects promoting the history of Delaware. A very special thanks to **GEORGE KENT, III** of the Delaware Department of Transportation for providing the base maps used in this publication. A special thanks to **AMY MAYO** of Aberdeen for her graphic design assistance in noting marker locations on the maps. A very special thanks to **LINDA BROWN** of the Wilmington Convention & Visitors Bureau for her help in showing a lost photographer where to go and who to talk to in New Castle County. A very special thanks to **J. HARRY FELDMAN** of the Wilmington Convention & Visitors Bureau for his assistance and support and in helping to write the section in the back on New Castle County. A very special thanks to **MARY SKELTON** of the Kent County Convention & Visitors Bureau for her assistance in helping us find important sites in Kent County and assisting us in writing the section on Kent County in the back of the book. A very special thanks to **PADDY DIETZ** of Nemours Mansion & Gardens for her efforts to get us permission to photograph the interiors of the mansion. A very special thanks to **DAVE BOARMAN, JR.** for his diligent efforts to make this book the best of the best and in completing the writing of the county's sections in the back of the book. A very special thanks to **LINDA FOSTER** for her assistance in doing contact work and supporting our efforts in doing this book.

JOE SWISHER and **ROGER MILLER**, 10-01-2001

CREDITS

Research by **Joe A. Swisher**
Text by **Joe A. Swisher**
Photography by **Roger Miller**
Design by **Roger Miller**
Editing by **Joe Swisher and Roger Miller**
Typesetting and Layouts by **Dave Boarman**

INFORMATION

ISBN# 0-911897-48-8 - (1st Edition)
Library of Congress Control Number: 2001096390
Printed in China

ORDERS

For direct orders please call or write for the specific pricing and the postage and handling to **IMAGE PUBLISHING, LTD**. Discounts are available for stores, institutions and corporations, with minimum order requirements. You may also contact us for sales through our web page. The suggested retail price at the time of publication is **US$24.95.**

The **State House** built in 1792 as the state capitol, witnessed the panorama of Delaware's political and social development during the early republic. It faces Dover's historic Green, a public area designated by William Penn in 1683 and the heart of Dover's historical district.

The **Kalmar Nyckel** replica was built in Wilmington at a shipyard on the Christiana River, around 350 years after the original. The **Kalmar Nyckel**, along with the ship *Vogle Grip*, brought the first European settlers in 1638 to what is now Wilmington. The settlers landed at "The Rocks." (See markers 39 and 90, pages 35 and 53)

TABLE OF CONTENTS

ACKNOWLEDGEMENT

SENATE LEADERSHIP

Left to right: Robert I. Marshall, Majority Whip
Thurman Adams, Jr., Majority Leader
Thomas B. Sharp, President Pro Tempore
Liane M. Sorenson, Minority Whip
Steven H. Amick, Minority Leader

HOUSE LEADERSHIP

Left to right: John F. VanSant, Minority Whip
Clifford G. Lee, Majority Whip
Wayne A. Smith, Majority Leader
Terry R. Spence, Speaker of the House
Robert F. Gilligan, Minority Leader

Since the passage of legislation establishing a state historical markers program in 1931, the Delaware General Assembly has continued to play a vital role in the program's success. Their ongoing support for this and other activities designed to promote a knowledge and awareness of Delaware's rich history and heritage, has made a major contribution towards the enhancement of the quality of life in the First State.

There is perhaps no better reflection of the continuing commitment of the General Assembly than the growing support for Delaware's historical markers program. With every new marker resulting from a request to legislators from their constituents, the program continues to remain responsive to the needs and interest of citizens from throughout the state. The Delaware General Assembly is to be congratulated for their support of this worthwhile endeavor.

FOREWORD
BY GOVERNOR RUTH ANN MINNER

Governor Ruth Ann Minner, born and raised on a small farm near Milford, was elected Delaware's first female governor in 2000. She served as lieutenant governor from 1993 to 2001 and was a member of the Delaware General Assembly from 1974 to 1992.

As Governor, I spend a fair amount of time crisscrossing Delaware by car. As I travel from place to place, I often spot the distinctive blue and yellow signs that are our historical markers. I can lean back and ponder the past of our great state and the remarkable stories behind each of those signs.

On the banks of the Brandywine River in New Castle County, one marker marks the birthplace of the Dupont Company, a world industrial leader and a dominant presence in our state for centuries. In Kent County, markers convey the life of Caesar Rodney, who rode on horseback through a rainstorm to Philadelphia to cast Delaware's vote for the Declaration of Independence. Rodney now appears on the Delaware quarter. In Wilmington, the introduction of the log cabin to the new world by Swedish settlers is commemorated among the steel and glass of a modern city skyline.

At Georgetown, a marker describes the unique and longstanding Delaware tradition of Return Day, when election results are announced and political candidates literally bury the hatchet two days after Election Day. Near Newark, the only battle ever fought on Delaware soil – that of Cooch's Bridge during the Revolutionary War – is marked and described as "pretty smart skirmishing."

From Aiken's Tavern in New Castle County to Zoar Methodist Church in Sussex County, this book catalogs Delaware's historical markers and Delaware's history. Each historical site described is distinctive and the events that took place on it unique. Together they create the tapestry from which our state's people and places, present and future are woven. I hope you will enjoy and learn from it as much as I have.

Ruth Ann Minner

The marker text reads:

OLD COURTHOUSE

Constructed in 1791 at the direction of the State Legislature, this structure served as the seat of Sussex County government until 1837, when it was sold and moved to this location to make way for the construction of the present County Court-house. It was later used as a private residence, and also served as a printing shop. On September 20, 1962, the building and lot were conveyed to the State of Delaware. A major renovation project was undertaken in 1974 with funding provided by the State and the National Park Service. The building was dedicated on Return Day in 1976, in honor of the nation's bicentennial.

SC-91

OLD COURTHOUSE, GEORGETOWN, SUSSEX COUNTY

Old Courthouse - A typical Delaware roadside marker noting the historical significance of an early Sussex County Courthouse that has been moved, restored and preserved as a state treasure. (See marker 70, page 113)

PREFACE

For over thirty years, it has been an annual event for my wife and me to leave our home in Maryland, in the beginning with our children and later with their families, and drive through Delaware on our way to the Atlantic Ocean beach resorts of Rehoboth, Bethany Beach or Ocean City for our annual vacation. As we passed through the small towns and rural countryside, I always marveled at the beauty of Delaware and wondered about its history. As we traveled, we would pass various Delaware Roadside Historical Markers, but never take the time to stop to read them. Over time, questions kept mounting, such as how many markers are there in Delaware and what are their themes? I looked for a book that might list the markers, but none was available. Eventually, I made a promise to myself that when I retired, I would dedicate some time to learning what I had missed all those years. This book is the result of my stopping to smell the roses in retirement. I hope you enjoy reading about Delaware as much as I enjoyed preparing the book with my good friend Roger Miller and my new friend in the Delaware Public Archives, Russ McCabe.

JOE A. SWISHER, AUTHOR

This is the second book I have completed with Joe Swisher. Joe has become a good friend and I can say that I have learned a lot about history and about myself from working with him. We began working on the Delaware book about three years ago. I didn't really think much about this project when I began: I knew Delaware. After all, I have been around the world eighteen times and I knew that Delaware consisted of Bethany Beach, Rehoboth Beach and the Delaware Memorial Bridge. Well, there was also this cute little town of New Castle somewhere by the bridge....

Someone wise once said, "It is only when you realize how little you know that you can truly learn." I didn't have a clue as to what Delaware was really like. As I began work on this book, my appreciation of Delaware exploded as I discovered one treasure after the next that I had never before been aware of. There are fantastic stories of patriotism to be discovered at numerous historic sites. At other historic sites, there are fascinating stories of industrial innovations which have made life better for us all. Then there are other sites which reflect the poignant stories of how people lived on farms, worshiped together, met, married and raised families of their own.

Not understanding the past keeps us from understanding the challenge and turmoil of the present. History is not about dusty museums and historic sites. History is understanding the achievements and successes of the past. Delaware, as you will see, is filled with some world-class historic sites. Nemours Mansion in Wilmington, for example, is a world-class site, the likes of which does not exist anywhere but perhaps in Europe. Winterthur is also one of the most superb sites and collections to be found anywhere in the world. The Hagley Museum is quite possibly the finest industrial museum in the world. At the State House in Dover you can walk on the same grounds where the citizens of the First State began the fight for liberty and freedom. Return Day in Georgetown is a celebration of American traditions as few Americans have experienced them in over fifty years: There are parades, flag-waving, the Governor, Representatives, babies and bands all set in the wondrous historic site of Georgetown. In the quiet town of Seaford, you will be amazed to find a completely restored 1840's farm known as the Governor Ross Mansion. These are just a few examples of some of the memorable historic sites to be seen and enjoyed in Delaware.

I do hope this book will help you find and enjoy some of the amazing historic sites available in Delaware. They reflect the achievements of some of the great men and women of Delaware. I hope your search will be as rewarding as mine has been.

ROGER MILLER, PHOTOGRAPHER

WILLIAM PENN STATUE, NEW CASTLE

William Penn arrived in New Castle in 1682 to lay claim to land that is now Delaware, granted to him by King Charles II and the Duke of York. (See marker 58, page 41)

INTRODUCTION

Delaware has an important place in the birth of our nation. There is no one book that would provide a total history of this great state, rather the history could be thought of as a series of individual events that, when taken together, create a mosaic of the historical heritage of Delaware. This book contains more than 300 concise stories about people, places and events that were deemed important enough by the citizens of Delaware to be commemorated with historical markers along the roads of the state.

The State of Delaware is located on 2,044 square miles of land that is mostly part of the low and flat Atlantic Coastal Plain that extends from New Jersey to Florida. It is located in the upper eastern side of a peninsula, with portions of Maryland and Virginia occupying the rest of the peninsula. Deriving its name from the three states which occupy it, this area is known as the Delmarva Peninsula. The northern part of Delaware is the beginning of the Piedmont Plateau and the highest elevation -448 feet- is located in the northeast part of the state. In Delaware, most rivers, streams and creeks empty into either the Delaware River or Bay; however the Nanticoke River and several small streams flow west into the Chesapeake Bay.

EARLY HISTORY

Native Americans lived in the Delaware area for hundreds of years before the European settlements were started. Members of the large Algonquin family of eastern tribes, they were composed of the Nanticoke, Choptank and Assateague in the south, and the "Delaware" or Lenni Lenape in the northern part of the state. The peninsula tribes were noted for being family oriented and peace loving people who hunted, fished and raised corn. They were often raided by the more aggressive Susquehannock Indians from the Susquehanna River Valley. While the native population steadily declined following European settlement, many members of these tribes continue to reside in Delaware today.

The modern history of Delaware begins with the early exploration of the East Coast of the United States. The Spaniards and Portuguese came first, in the sixteenth century. Then, in 1609, the English explorer and navigator Henry Hudson was hired by the Dutch to find a shorter passage to Asia. During his voyage in the ship *Half Moon*, he explored the Delaware Bay and the Hudson River. In 1610, a sea captain named Samuel Argall, from the English colony Virginia, was blown off course and sailed into a bay which he named after the governor of Virginia, Sir Thomas West, a nobleman whose title was Lord de la Warr. It is doubtful that Lord de la Warr ever saw or explored the bay, river and state which bear his name. Other Dutch explorers were Cornelius May (who is credited with naming Cape May, New Jersey) in 1613 and Cornelius Hendricksen in 1614.

In 1631, eleven years after the landing of the English pilgrims at Plymouth, Massachusetts, the first settlement of Europeans was made on Delaware soil. A group of Dutchmen formed a trading company headed by Captain David Pietersen de Vries. The expedition of about 30 individuals sailed from the town of Hoorn under the leadership of Captain Peter Heyes in the ship the *Walvis* (Whale). Their settlement, Zwaanendael, meaning "valley of swans," was located near the present town of Lewes on the west bank of the Lewes Creek. Establishment of this early settlement preceded the British land grant and initial settlement of Maryland by the Calverts (Lord Baltimore) by one year and was the deciding event which later influenced the location of the eastern boundaries of Maryland and hence the size of the current State of Delaware.

Arriving in the New World in 1632 to visit the colony, Captain de Vries found the settlers had been killed and their buildings burned following an apparent dispute with a local Indian tribe. The settlement is commemorated by the Zwaanendael Museum in Lewes.

No further attempts at colonization were made on Delaware soil until 1638, when the Swedes established their colony at the site of the present day city of Wilmington, the first permanent settlement in Delaware. The first Swedish expedition consisted of two ships, *Kalmar Nyckel* (Key of Kalmar) and *Vogel Grip*, under the leadership of Peter Minuit. The location of the first Swedish settlement was at "The Rocks," on the Christina River, near the foot of Seventh Street. A fort, called Fort Christina, after the young queen of Sweden, was built and

The Old Guard Fife and Drum Corps, United States Army, 3rd Infantry Regiment, Fort Myer, Virginia, participating in the Return Day parade at Georgetown. (See marker 80, page 119)

the river was likewise named for her. Although this initial effort was a joint venture between the Swedes and the Dutch, the Dutch withdrew to concentrate on the New Amsterdam colony (New York) and what is now New Jersey. The Dutch called their colony New Netherland and the Swedes called theirs New Sweden.

As time went on, the Dutch became alarmed at the growing strength of the Swedish colony and wanted to add it to their New Netherland colony. To reclaim the Delaware area, the Dutch built Fort Casimir in 1651, at the site of present day New Castle.

The most important Swedish governor was Colonel Johan Printz, who ruled the colony under Swedish law for ten years, from 1643 to 1653. Johan Rising replaced Colonel Printz. Upon the arrival of Rising in 1654, the Dutch post, Fort Casimir was seized. Rising governed the Swedish colony from his headquarters at Fort Christina until the autumn of 1655, when Peter Stuyvesant came from New Amsterdam with a Dutch fleet, subjugated the Swedish forts, and established the authority of the colony of New Netherlands throughout the area formerly controlled by the colony of New Sweden. Although this marked the end of Swedish rule in Delaware, cultural, social and religious influences of these Swedish settlers has had a lasting effect upon the lives of the people in this area and upon subsequent westward migrations of many generations. Old Swedes (Holy Trinity) Church, built by the Swedes in Wilmington in 1698, was supplied by the mother church with missionaries until after the Revolution. It is one of the oldest Protestant churches in North America. Fort Christina State Park in Wilmington, with the fine monument created by noted sculptor, Carl Milles, and presented by the people of Sweden, perpetuates the memory of these first settlers and preserves "The Rocks" where they first landed.

Following the seizure of the colony of New Sweden, the Dutch restored the name Fort Casimir and made it the principal settlement of the South River, as contrasted with the North or Hudson River. In a short time the area within the fort could no longer accommodate all the settlers, and a town, named New Amstel (now New Castle), was laid out.

During this early period, England had colonies both north and south of New Netherlands. In 1664, the British, continuing their efforts to gain control of the colonies on the East Coast, came up the Delaware Bay, captured New Amstel, and renamed it New Castle. The Delaware settlements became British territory under the control of the Duke of York. As a result of this military action, the British King, Charles II, also granted all territory east of the Delaware River (now New Jersey) to his brother, James, Duke of York.

The year 1681 marked the granting of the Province of Pennsylvania to William Penn by King Charles II and the arrival of Penn's agents on the Delaware River. They soon reported to the proprietor that the new province would be land locked if the colonies on either side of the Delaware River or Bay were hostile. The English Crown owned New Jersey, Pennsylvania and Delaware at this time. The King, not wanting to infringe on the Duke of York's territory, ordered a curved, northern boundary be drawn within a 12-mile radius of the spire of the old New Castle Courthouse for the Delaware area. Further, the area defined within the arch would include the Delaware River over to the New Jersey shore at low tide as a part of Delaware. As one goes south in the river below the 12-mile radius, the boundary between New Jersey and Delaware is at the center of the body of water. This action by the King allowed Pennsylvania to have land on the Delaware River for the creation of a port.

As a result of Penn's petition to the Crown for land on the west side of the Delaware River or Bay below his province, the Duke of York, in March 1682, conveyed to William Penn, by deeds and leases (now exhibited by the Delaware Public Archives in the Hall of Records at Dover), the land included in the counties of New Castle, St. Jones and Deale. On October 27, of the same year, William Penn landed in America at New Castle and there took possession from the Duke of York's agents as proprietor of the Three Lower Counties on Delaware. On this occasion, the colonists subscribed an oath of allegiance to the new proprietor, and the first General Assembly of Pennsylvania was formed with the territories having full privileges under Penn's famous "Frame of Government." Also in that year, the counties of St. Jones and Deale were renamed Kent and Sussex Counties. Hereafter, the Delaware counties were called the Three Lower Counties on Delaware or the Lower Counties.

In the early years of William Penn's government of the Three Lower Counties on Delaware, each county was divided into areas called "hundreds." This term was applied to all areas within the Delaware counties and is somewhat analogous to townships in Pennsylvania. The first mention of the term

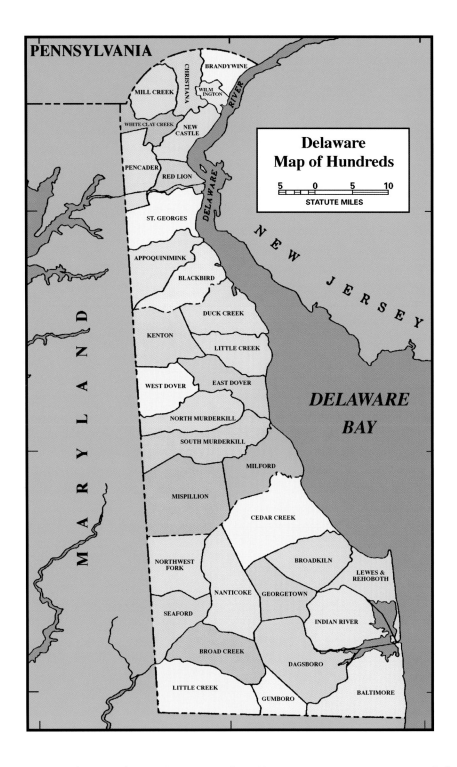

Delaware Hundreds - In the early years of William Penn's government of the "Three Lower Counties on Delaware," the counties were divided into areas called "hundreds." The "hundreds" were tax assessment districts with some responsibility for self-government.

hundred in Delaware was in 1690, when the Provincial Council instructed the magistrates and grand juries of the counties to divide the counties into hundreds. The designating of hundreds in England was supposed to be related to an area having ten families, assuming each family was comprised of ten persons, making a total of one hundred individuals. In England the hundreds were governed by a High Constable and had its own court. In Delaware counties, they were utilized as a civil subdivision of convenience for administration, tax assessment, and possibly defense purposes. In the 1890's, Delaware incorporated the old hundreds into their election districts. Today, the records associated with hundreds are housed in the Delaware Public Archives in Dover and are used as research sources for genealogy and early history studies.

Pennsylvania was settled as a predominately Quaker colony. The Quakers were pacifists and were opposed to military service and warfare, preferring to settle disputes through discussions and compromise. As a result, the colony did not want to build up the militia to defend the Lower Counties from raids from privateers and pirates. This is one reason William Penn, in 1704, agreed to let the Lower Counties have their own assembly at New Castle.

After 1682, a long dispute ensued between William Penn and Lord Baltimore of the Province of Maryland as to the exact dominion controlled by Penn in The Lower Counties on Delaware. Most of present day Delaware was originally claimed by Lord Baltimore when in 1632 he sent his first colonist to Maryland to start settlement on his earlier land grant from the King of England. His charter stated that he would own to the Delaware River provided no other colonies were there. When the Dutch, in 1631, started a colony (which was destroyed by the Indians within a year) near what is now Lewes, the settlement became a part of the argument that the boundaries of Maryland should not extend all the way to the Delaware River. However, until this was resolved after many years in the Courts of England, Lord Baltimore did grant land to settlers in what is now within the boundaries of Delaware. When the matter was resolved, the land grants given by Lord Baltimore were upheld. The boundary was settled by giving both Maryland and Penn's Three Lower Counties (now Delaware) half the peninsula between the Chesapeake and Delaware Bays in the north-south direction.

Between 1763 and 1768, the noted English scientists Charles Mason and Jeremiah Dixon surveyed Delaware's boundaries along with the northern boundary of Maryland. The southern east-west boundary of Delaware was intended to be closer to Lewes. However an earlier survey party misjudged a land form as being Cape Henlopen, and started their survey at what is now Fenwick Island, heading west in a straight line from their Crownstone. The western Delaware boundary is not a straight line, but has a slight bow in Delaware's favor in the northern part. This bow is a continuation of the circle formed by the twelve-mile radius from the spire of the old New Castle Courthouse.

When one looks at the area where the Pennsylvania, Maryland and Delaware lines connect, there is a notch off the circular boundary and one can visualize a triangular piece of land of about 800 acres that could have been allocated to any of the three states. This area is commonly referred to as "The Wedge." Legend has it that in the early days this area was a "no-man's-land," not formally claimed or governed by any state. It was even rumored that it was a "safe haven" for outlaws because no existing lawmen felt he had official jurisdiction in that area. The ownership of this area was disputed for many years between Pennsylvania and Delaware. The Mason and Dixon Survey designated it as a part of Pennsylvania, but this was not accepted by Delaware. The ownership problem was not resolved until 1893, when the courts awarded Delaware this land.

In 1774, Caesar Rodney, Thomas McKean and George Read represented the Delaware counties at the First Continental Congress in Philadelphia, which petitioned Parliament and the King for tax relief. In April 1775, a confrontation between British troops and a band of colonial militia occurred at Lexington, Massachusetts, and thereafter, the colonies began to arm for war. In the spring of 1776, McKean, Read and Rodney attended the Second Continental Congress, which started the colonies on their bold resolution to be independent. On the first vote for independence, McKean voted for independence and Read was opposed. Caesar Rodney was not present for the first vote, but upon hearing of the deadlock, he traveled non-stop, pausing only to change horses, and reached Philadelphia in time to cast his vote for independence. On July 4, the Delaware delegation

Amish Farmer - In the early twentieth century, an Amish settlement was established in Kent County around Dover, Delaware. Today, the community is an integral part of the Delaware's vibrant agricultural industry. The Amish still farm with the same techniques as in the early 1900's.

signified their approval of the Declaration of Independence. At the time of the Declaration of Independence, Delaware not only declared itself free from the British Empire, but also established, in September 1776, a state government entirely separate from Pennsylvania, hence becoming known as Delaware State. (The official name was changed to the State of Delaware in 1792.)

With the advent of the Revolution, nearly 4,000 men enlisted for service from the small State of Delaware. The colonial wars had built up the militia system and supplied a number of capable officers who led Delaware troops in all the principal engagements from the Battle of Long Island to the Siege of Yorktown. The only Revolutionary engagement fought on Delaware soil was the Battle of Cooch's Bridge, near Newark, on September 3, 1777.

In 1786, John Dickinson of Delaware presided over the Annapolis Convention, which preceded the Federal Constitutional Convention that met in Philadelphia the following year. Delaware was the first of the thirteen original states to ratify the Constitution of the United States. This unanimous ratification took place at a convention in Dover, at a tavern because there were no state government buildings there at that time. On December 7, 1787, Delaware became "The First State" of the new Federal Union. Proud of this heritage, Delawareans continue to honor the traditions that made them the first state to ratify the United States Constitution, the document that continues to protect our nation's justice, strength and liberty.

MARKER PROGRAM HISTORY

The Delaware Historical Marker Program began in 1930, when the governor appointed a commission to review the historical places and events in Delaware and propose a way to identify them. In early January 1931, the commission proposed several types of markers and a number of historical sites that should be identified by this means. The commission also proposed the plan of marking the boundaries of the old "hundreds" in Kent and Sussex Counties as a means of preserving the Anglo-Saxon political divisions. The plan was not adopted for New Castle County, as the old "hundreds" and the legislative districts were identical at that time.

In April 1931, the General Assembly of Delaware passed an act establishing a permanent commission to erect historic markers throughout the state and authorized funds to support their initial efforts.

By October 1931, the five-person commission was appointed and organized for work. The commission decided to erect two types of markers: (1) bronze tablets affixed to houses, walls or boulders, and (2) cast-iron highway markers supported on cast-iron posts. On the markers would be the seal of the state enclosed in a diamond shape. By July 1, 1933, the commission had erected 152 highway markers. The markers in each county were numbered sequentially as they were proposed, preceded by NC, K or S to note the county in which they were located. Since the beginning of the program in the 1930's, the State of Delaware has erected over 400 markers. Some of these markers have duplicate texts and are placed on approaches to municipalities or areas of special interest, such as the hundreds. As many are roadside markers, there has been some attrition due to automobile collisions, road changes and other events.

Since 1990, the State Historical Markers Program has been administered by the Delaware Public Archives. During the past decade the number of new markers being installed has continued to grow, and the program is as active today as it was in the 1930's. This recent growth has been fueled by a broader interest in the history of the state's communities and the people and institutions which have shaped their history. This book attempts to document all historical markers and many of the bronze tablets, whether they are still standing or not. All the stories are part of the historic mosaic of Delaware.

LOCATION

The location of the markers is addressed by two means in the book. First, all known markers are categorized as being in one of the three Delaware counties. Each county's markers are addressed separately, with each section containing a county map showing the relative locations of the markers within the county. Some maps of municipalities are also included to further note the location of markers. Secondly, at the end of the text of each marker is a brief description of the general location where one should be able to find the marker if it still exists. I did not have the luxury of being able to travel to each location to verify the actual existence of each marker.

Caesar Rodney's Statue is located in the center of downtown Wilmington, directly across the street from the Hotel du Pont. This statue represents his ride to Philadelphia to break the deadlock in the Delaware Delegation to approve the Declaration of Independence. A likeness of this statue is found on the state commemorative quarters issued by the U.S. Mint. (See marker 8, page 65)

MARKER TEXT

The text of each marker reproduced in this publication is solely of the actual wording. Many of the sentences in the text are very long, with little punctuation used. Each text was faithfully reproduced as written, but sometimes the sources were difficult to decipher. Any misspellings in the text are provided as presented.

The accuracy of the text of some markers could be questioned. Many of the markers refer to places or events that occurred hundreds of years earlier. However, the texts of the markers were developed by caring people to preserve for future generations their most accurate recollections of times passed. With this in mind, the modern reader can capture a glimpse of Delaware history from the markers in order to begin to form a reasonably accurate picture of the heritage of the state. If one needs greater accuracy, there are other research sources available to complete the picture.

The majority of the texts are from roadside historical markers mounted on metal poles. Some are from bronze plaques mounted on buildings, walls or boulders. The latter are noted as bronze plaques at the end of the location texts for the markers.

HOW TO USE THE BOOK

In each county, the markers are alphabetized based on the first important word in the title. The intent is that if you are motoring down a street or highway and pass a marker, you can read the first important word and look up the text in the book easily without backtracking. Of course, this assumes that you know the county you are in at the time.

For each county there is a map locating the approximate position of the markers. Each marker is numbered with a number in a circle, corresponding to the estimated location on the area map. The marker numbers with a red background on the map are believed to be still standing. The marker numbers with the green background probably no longer exist. The title of each marker is next and helps to describe the site. The historical text follows, then the general location. At the end of the location text, in parenthesis, is either the state-assigned marker number mentioned earlier or the designation Bronze Tablet (which are unnumbered). Finally, if an M follows the state number, it designates that the marker is probably missing.

To challenge you as you search for and discover the fascinating information in the historical markers, there is a list of questions on pages 142 and 143. Some examples of these are: Who ordered Dover to be laid out as a town? What does "kill" mean in Dutch? What happened at "The Rocks?" To assist you we have provided the page and marker number where the answer can be found.

If any reader of this book finds a mistake in an existing text of a marker or its location, please send the information to the author in care of Image Publishing, Ltd., 1411 Hollins Street, Baltimore, Maryland 21223. Further, if anyone finds a historical plaque he thinks should be in future editions of this publication, please send a copy of the text and location of the plaque to the address above.

To the first person who finds and notifies me of a legitimate Delaware Historical Marker on a pole not included in this book but installed by the state **before** 31 December 2000, I will send a free copy of this book or the reprinted book (Note: markers numbered NC 112, K 70 and S 140, and higher were installed after 31 December 2000). The first person to notify me of a unique and significant bronze plaque relating to Delaware history, which I deem to be important enough to add to future editions of this book, will also receive a complimentary copy of the reprinted book.

BIBLIOGRAPHY

Beach, Jack. *Pirates on the Delaware.*
 Lewes: Media Associates, ©1993

Delaware, Small Wonder (Doc.#10-03-95-09-01)

Delaware Tourism Office, The Delaware Travel Guide,
 Baltimore: Media Two, n.d.

Federal Writer's Project for the State of Delaware.
 Delaware, a Guide to the First State.
 New York: The Viking Press, ©1938.

Hoffecker, Carol E. *Delaware, a Bicentennial History.*
 New York: W. W. Norton & Co., Inc., ©1977.

Hoffecker, Carol E. *Delaware, the First State.*
 Wilmington: The Middle Atlantic Press, ©1988.

Lunt, Dudley. *The Bounds of Delaware.*
 Wilmington: The Star Publishing Co., ©1947.

Munroe, John A. *Colonial Delaware, a History.*
 Millwood: The KTO Press, ©1978.

Munroe, John A. *History of Delaware.*
 Newark: University of Delaware Press, ©1993.

The **Old Court House** on Delaware Street, New Castle, was built in 1732 and is the oldest surviving government building in Delaware. The Colonial Assembly utilized the building until 1777, when Dover became the capital of Delaware.

NEW CASTLE COUNTY

① AIKEN'S TAVERN

Site of old Aiken's Tavern. Quarters of General William Howe, September 3 to 8, 1777. Tavern then owned by Mathew Aiken, who laid out this village, naming it Aikentown. Renamed for Glasgow in Scotland.

DE 896, east side, near US 40, at Glasgow near Methodist Episcopal Church. (NC 43)

② AMERICAN POSITION

The Americans at Battle of Cooch's Bridge, September 3, 1777, were stationed along road between here and Aikentown [Glasgow]. They had a post at Cooch's Mill which stood on west side of creek, where severe fighting occurred. Skirmishing began near Aikentown and continued over Iron Hill to Welsh Baptist Meeting House.

Old Baltimore Pike (Rd. 336), north side, east end of Cooch's Bridge, 3.5 miles from Newark. (NC 41M)

③ ANTHONY - DELAWARE'S FIRST KNOWN BLACK SETTLER

A black man named Anthony was among the first permanent settlers of New Sweden. He came to the colony from the West Indies in 1639 aboard the Swedish ship *Vogel Grip*. Records indicate that Black Anthony became a free man named Antoni Swart, an employee of Governor Johan Printz, who cut hay and sailed Printz's sloop during the 1640's and 1650's.

Fort Christina Park, Wilmington. (NC 80)

④ APPOQUINIMINK FRIENDS MEETING HOUSE

Believed to be one of the smallest Quaker Meeting Houses in the nation, the Appoquinimink Friends Meeting House was built in 1785 by David Wilson and presented to the Friends as a gift. Local tradition identifies this structure as a stop on the Underground Railroad during the years preceding the Civil War. While en route to destinations north of Delaware, runaway slaves would hide in the loft of the church in order to escape capture. Prominent local Quakers who served as agents on the railroad included John Alston and John Hunn. The Appoquinimink Friends Meeting House was placed on the National Register of Historic Places in 1972.

DE 299, south side, 0.8 mile west of US 1, Odessa. (NC 90)

⑤ ASBURY METHODIST EPISCOPAL CHURCH

Organized about the year 1769. Early meetings held in Academy Woods, Gilpin's Wharf and Thelwell's School. Church built 1789. Dedicated by Bishop Francis Asbury. Here is buried Allen McLane, lieutenant in Caesar Rodney's regiment 1775; captain of Dragoons 1777; leader of charge in taking Paulus Hook [Jersey City] 1779; major in Washington's Army at Yorktown 1781 and commandant of Veteran Corps in War of 1812.

South-east corner of Third and Walnut Streets, Wilmington. [Bronze Tablet]

⑥ ASHLEY MANSION

Ashton Richardson built Ashley Mansion in 1804 on land he inherited from his father. A prominent Quaker, Ashton Richardson owned several milling operations and was considered one of the most eligible bachelors in the area. After marrying in 1807, Richardson and his wife Mary occupied the house until their deaths in the early 1850's. Ashley Mansion remained in the Richardson family until 1899, when the property was sold. In 1916 the house was purchased by Jefferson D. Chalfant, the acclaimed still-life painter. Chalfant used one wing of the house for a studio, where he produced many of the works that brought him

INTERIOR, OLD COURT HOUSE, NEW CASTLE

INTERIOR, OLD COURT HOUSE, NEW CASTLE

INTERIOR, OLD COURT HOUSE, NEW CASTLE

The city of New Castle served as the seat of government of "the Three Lower Counties" from 1704 to 1777. The **Old Court House** has been restored to its eighteenth century appearance.

national attention.

DE 4 (Maryland Avenue) and Ashton Place, east entrance, west of Wilmington, south of Eismere. (NC 96)

7 **BATTLE OF COOCH'S BRIDGE**

American light infantry and cavalry under General William Maxwell encountered advance guard of British and Hessian troops under Generals Howe, Cornwallis, and Knyphausen in this vicinity September 3, 1777. American troops were expert marksmen drafted by General Washington from several brigades of his army then encamped near Wilmington. Only battle of American Revolution on Delaware soil and claimed to have been the first in which the Stars and Stripes were carried. Erected by the patriotic societies and citizens of the State of Delaware, September 3, 1901. Inscription revised by Historic Markers Commission, 1932.

Old Baltimore Pike (Rd. 336), 3.5 miles south of Newark, 4.5 miles from Christiana. [Bronze Tablet]

8 **THE BEAR**

Near this spot stood the old Bear Tavern. Used from colonial times until 1845, when old building was destroyed. Generals Washington and Lafayette, and many other famous people used this inn in their passage north and south to and from Chesapeake Bay.

US 40, north side, four miles west of US 13. (NC 57M)

9 **BETHEL A. M. E. CHURCH**

On May 10, 1846, a group of African-American residents of Wilmington who had affiliated themselves with the African Methodist Episcopal Church held a meeting for the purpose of electing trustees and organizing as a corporate body. At the time, approximately 15 families were meeting from house to house, worshiping under the direction of ministers from Mother Bethel A. M. E. Church in Philadelphia. The following September, the congregation purchased land at 12th and Elizabeth Streets on which a church was to be erected. The new structure was dedicated in April 1847.

In 1853 the congregation relocated to a site at 6th and Penn Streets. They continued to worship there until 1865, when their need for a larger building led them to purchase the present site, where the Zion Evangelical German Lutheran Church then stood. The old building was used until 1878, when it was demolished and a new structure was built here.

A tragic fire led to the complete destruction of the church on New Year's Day, 1935. On March 5, 1939, the members of Bethel A. M. E. Church dedicated their new house of worship. The church was expanded in 1976 with the opening of the adjoining multipurpose building.

Corner of 6th and Walnut Streets, Wilmington. (NC 102)

10 **BETHEL CHURCH**

Site of Bethel Church, a branch of Welsh Tract Baptist Church at the foot of Iron Hill. Originated about 1780 by Rev. John Boggs at the house of David Morton. Church erected 1786 at instance of Messrs. Porter and Lewden. Land donated by Andrew and Ebenezer Morton. Services discontinued about 1871.

DE 273 [Hare's Corner to Christiana], north side, one mile west of US 40. (NC 56M)

11 **BLOCK HOUSE**

Used for defense against Indians. Tradition says built 1654 by John Risingh, Governor colony of New Sweden. Taken by Dutch 1655 under Peter Stuyvesant. Attacked by Indians 1671. Captured by British 1777. Only house remaining of original settlement on Naaman's Creek.

US 13, west side, four tenths mile south of the DE-PA State Line. (NC 1M)

NEW CASTLE ON THE DELAWARE RIVER

IMMANUEL CHURCH, NEW CASTLE

THE GREEN, NEW CASTLE

OLD ARSENAL, NEW CASTLE

New Castle, located on the Delaware River, was Delaware's colonial capital. Step back in time, experience the charm and beauty by walking the cobblestone streets, and enjoy the historic sites. The **Old Arsenal**, located on the Green, was built in 1809 by the Federal Government in anticipation of the War of 1812. (See marker 42 and 72, pages 37 and 47) **Immanuel Church**, also located on the Green, has a cemetery which contains the graves of many prominent Delawareans.

12 BRANDYWINE VILLAGE

Around 1740 water-powered mills began to appear in this area where the Brandywine River ends its journey - falling 124 feet in its final five miles. Small vessels carrying grain from nearby farms sailed directly to the mills. Other ships laden with flour sailed away to distant markets where Brandywine Superfine Flour was known for its high quality.

In 1799 residents of the community erected a handsome building to serve as a community hall and school. By 1820 several fine millers' homes overlooked Market Street. The village was home to coopers, carpenters, blacksmiths, leather workers, and mill hands. In 1869 Brandywine Village became part of Wilmington. Brandywine Village was listed in the National Register of Historic Places in 1971. The boundaries of the district were expanded in 1976. Well-preserved millers' houses, the Academy, and especially the sound of the rushing Brandywine, remain as reminders of a rich past.

Corner of Market and Race Streets, Wilmington. (NC 101)

13 BRITISH POSITION

British and Hessian regiments were advancing along this road September 3, 1777, when "pretty smart skirmishing" occurred between them and the Americans. British and Hessian armies progressed until their lines extended from Aiken's Tavern [Glasgow] to Iron Hill and across the Christiana, where they remained for five days.

DE 896, west side, two-tenths mile south of Cooch's Bridge. (NC 42M)

14 BROAD DYKE

Original dyke built by Dutch 1655. Center of twelve mile circle marking top of Delaware, surveyed 1701, by Empson and Pusey.

Chestnut and Third Streets, north-west corner, New Castle. (NC 22)

15 BUENA VISTA

Built in 1845 by John M. Clayton (1796-1856). Secretary of State in President Taylor's cabinet. He also served Delaware as U. S. Senator, jurist and Secretary of State. He drafted the Clayton-Bulwer Treaty, which eventually guaranteed that the Panama Canal would be open to ships of all nations. The house is now a state museum.

US 13, east side of highway, near Rd. 380, nine miles south of Wilmington. (NC 15)

16 BUENA VISTA

Built 1842 by John M. Clayton. He was born 1796 at Dagsboro. Secretary of State and Chief Justice of Delaware. United States Senator three times, Secretary of State of United States under two presidents. Negotiated Clayton-Bulwer Treaty with Great Britain. Died 1856. Buried in old Presbyterian Church Yard, Dover.

US 13, nine miles south of Wilmington. [Bronze Tablet]

17 CAESAR RODNEY'S CAMP, 1777

In this vicinity was the Noxentown camp of Delaware militia under command of Caesar Rodney, September, 1777, when British under Howe invaded northern Delaware from Head of Elk on their march to Philadelphia. From near here Caesar Rodney was in correspondence with Washington before and after Battle of Brandywine.

North side of road running east from DE 71 at Noxentown Lake, south of Middletown. (NC 48M)

18 CAMP BRANDYWINE

In the Civil War the first camp of this name was at Wilmington Fair Grounds for the First and Second Delaware Regiments. The same name was given this site in September, 1862, for a camp of Pennsylvania troops sent to guard powder mills. They were relieved by the Fourth Delaware

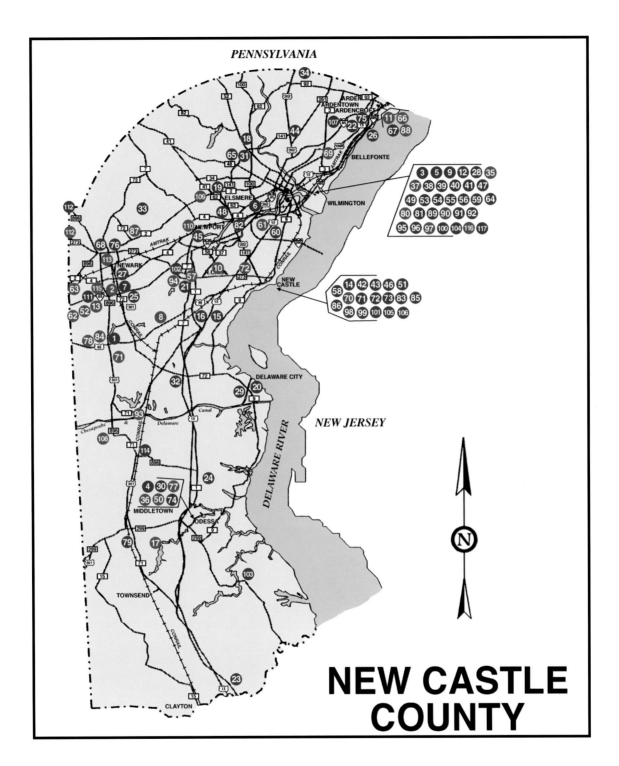

PENNSYLVANIA

PENNSYLVANIA

ARDEN
ARDENTOWN
ARDENCROFT
BELLEFONTE
WILMINGTON
ELSMERE
NEWPORT
NEWARK
NEW CASTLE
DELAWARE CITY
NEW JERSEY
DELAWARE RIVER
Chesapeake & Delaware Canal
MIDDLETOWN
ODESSA
TOWNSEND
CLAYTON

N

NEW CASTLE COUNTY

New Castle County is the northern-most county in Delaware and borders Maryland on the west, Pennsylvania on the north, and New Jersey on the east. The county is a hub for commerce, manufacturing and transportation activities. Complimenting the county are educational institutions, magnificent estates and historical sites.

Regiment the next month when the site was known briefly as Camp DuPont then later as Camp Brandywine.

DE 52 and DE 141, near Greenville Shopping Center. (NC 78)

 CAMP DUPONT

First established May, 1861. The Fourth Regiment Delaware Volunteer Infantry camped here June to October, 1862, whence they moved to a camp of the same name near Kenneth Pike. The remustered First Delaware Regiment camped here in early February, 1864, following a 30-day furlough before returning to active service in Virginia. The camp was named to honor Rear Admiral Samuel F. Du Pont.

DE 41 and DE 34 [Faulkland Road], Brandywine Springs Park. (NC 79)

20 CHRIST EPISCOPAL CHURCH
DELAWARE CITY

In 1847, the Reverend Andrew F. Freeman and the Reverend Thomas F. Billop were appointed as a committee to organize and solicit subscriptions for a Protestant Episcopal church in Delaware City. The parish was formally organized on May 28, 1848, when Bishop Alfred Lee officiated for the first time to a numerous congregation assembled in the Methodist Church. The church was officially admitted into the full union at the following Diocesan Convention. A house of worship was provided by the Commissioners of Public School District #76, who authorized the use of the school house.

On February 16, 1849, the congregation purchased this property from John Ashhurst. Construction of the church was commenced in April of that year. On February 22, 1851, the first worship service was held. The church was formally consecrated by Bishop Lee on December 13, 1857. Parish tradition contends that the design for the building was based upon that of the Church of the Redeemer for Seaman, an

ornate floating edifice which served the needs of Port of Philadelphia sailors from 1849 to 1853.

The building of a rectory was authorized on February 7, 1870. The structure was completed the following November. Construction of the Parish Hall was completed in 1895. The building was occupied and dedicated at a service of benediction conducted by Bishop Leighton Coleman on June 23 of that year. Following the completion of much-needed renovations and repairs, Christ Church was formally reopened on October 31, 1920.

Corner of 3rd and Clinton Streets, Delaware City. (NC 100)

 CHRISTIANA UNITED METHODIST CHURCH

The origin of this congregation may be traced to the earliest days of Methodism in America. In March, 1771, Joseph Pilmore, one of the first Methodist missionaries from England, preached outdoors at Christiana. Upon returning in 1773, Reverend Pilmore noted the enthusiastic response of local residents to the message and philosophy of church founder John Wesley. As a result of these early efforts, a "Society" of local Methodists was organized. Many of the first meetings were held in the homes of members.

In October, 1807, a meeting of interested persons was held at the home of William Wright for the purposes of organizing themselves into a corporate body, and planning for construction of "Salem Meeting House." In 1827, Christiana residents who had worshipped at Salem, bought a house from S. Johnson, which they dismantled and rebuilt on land purchased by them on the Christiana-Stanton Road. The first sermon was given by Rev. James Ayers in September of that year.

On July 9,1857, the Trustees of the Christiana Methodist Episcopal Church purchased land here from Abraham and Mary Cannon "in trust" that they "cause to be erected" a new place of worship. The present church was constructed in

GEORGE READ II HOUSE

INTERIOR - READ HOUSE

INTERIOR - READ HOUSE

INTERIOR - READ HOUSE

George Read II House and Gardens - George Read II (1765-1836) was a prominent lawyer and son of a signer of the Declaration of Independence. The stately 22 room house, built in 1801 on the banks of the Delaware River in the colonial town of New Castle, recalls the elegance of times past.

that year at a cost of $4,000. Plans were prepared by Rev. James Hand. The building was dedicated by Bishop Levi Scott on January 28, 1858. Civil War casualties are among the oldest graves in the adjoining cemetery.

21 West Main Street, Christiana. (NC 98)

22 CLAYMONT STONE SCHOOL

Also known as Naaman's Creek School # 1, the Claymont Stone School was built on land donated by John Dickinson, the "Penman of the American Revolution," in 1805. The building was expanded and renovated in 1905. Evidence suggests that it may have been the first racially integrated public school in the state. The Claymont Stone School was listed in the National Register of Historic Places in 1990.

West side of US 13, approximately 1/3 mile south of US 13 and I-495, Claymont. (NC 105)

23 CLEARFIELD FARM

Built in the mid-eighteenth century by Captain David Clark, Clearfield Farm was the home of his grandson John Clark [1761-1821], Governor of Delaware from 1817-1820. John Clark served as colonel in the Delaware militia and as Justice of the Peace before being elected governor in 1816. After his term expired, Clark moved into the town of Smyrna to become President of the Commercial Bank of Smyrna. Following his death, the property was inherited by his granddaughters. Local folklore identifies the plantation as a stop on the Underground Railroad. The property was listed on the National Register of Historic Places in 1973.

Rd. 485 (Smyrna Landing Road) and Rd. 30 (Paddock Road) east of DE 1 and north of Smyrna, on grounds of Delaware Correctional Center. (NC 89)

24 COMMODORE THOMAS MACDONOUGH

Early home of Commodore Thomas MacDonough. Hero of Battle of Lake Champlain 1814. Born 1783. Died 1825. Commodore 1813. Assisted Commodore Decatur in capturing and burning the "Philadelphia" off the coast of Tripoli, 1804. Original name of village "The Trap," changed to "McDonough" 1814. His parents lie in old burying ground nearby.

US 13, west side, south of Rd. 15 (DE 896), 20 miles south of Wilmington. (NC 16)

25 COOCH HOUSE

Erected 1760 by Thomas Cooch who had come here from England 1746. He was captain in French and Indian War, member of Colonial Assembly, judge of Court of Common Pleas and colonel in American Revolution. House enlarged by his grandson, William Cooch, an incorporator of first Chesapeake and Delaware Canal Company, and Major General of Delaware militia. Lord Cornwallis had quarters here September 3 to 8, 1777.

Old Baltimore Pike (Rd. 336), north side, 3.5 miles south of Newark. [Bronze Tablet]

26 THE DARLEY HOUSE

The home of world-renowned illustrator Felix O. C. Darley [1822-1888]. Built in the late 18th century and enlarged several times during the first half of the 19th century, the house was purchased by Darley in 1863 and renamed "The Wren's Nest." During his career, Darley illustrated books for Washington Irving, Edgar Allen Poe, Nathaniel Hawthorne, Charles Dickens, and James Fenimore Cooper. Two of his most notable works were Irving's *The Legend of Sleepy Hollow* and *Rip Van Winkle*. Charles Dickens visited here for two weeks during his triumphant tour of America in 1867. The house was placed on the National Register of Historic Places in 1974.

3701 Philadelphia Pike (US 13), Claymont. (NC 91)

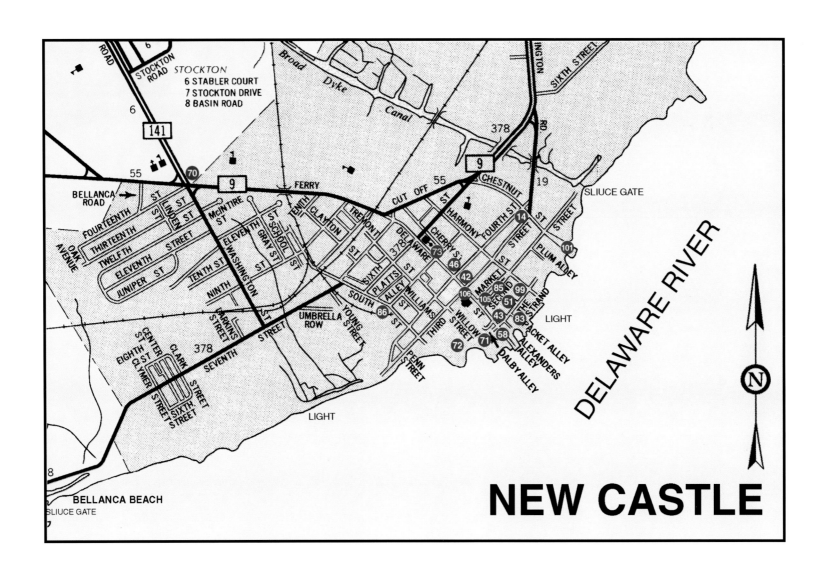

STOCKTON
6 STABLER COURT
7 STOCKTON DRIVE
8 BASIN ROAD

NEW CASTLE

New Castle is a well-preserved colonial town with many elegant 18th century residences.

DEER PARK HOTEL

Since the mid-18th century an establishment for public hospitality has existed here. The first building, of wood construction, was known as St. Patrick's Inn. Famous visitors included surveyors Mason and Dixon. The property was purchased by James S. Martin in 1847, and the core of the present structure was erected by him circa 1851. The new building was named the Deer Park Hotel.

The coming of the railroad to Newark resulted in an increased demand for hotel and tavern accommodations. In the last quarter of the 19th century the building was expanded and otherwise improved. During its colorful past the Deer Park has provided the community with an array of social spaces. In addition to offering refreshments and lodging, the Deer Park has been used at various times as a public meeting place, ballroom, polling place, barbershop, and women's seminary. It continues to serve as a popular gathering place for college students, faculty, and other townspeople. In 1982 the Deer Park Hotel was listed in the National Register of Historic Places.

108 West Main Street, Newark. (NC 106)

 DELAWARE BANK BUILDING

The first Bank of Delaware, organized 1795, and located originally at northeast corner of Fourth and Market Streets, erected this building at Sixth and Market Streets, 1816. Used continuously until 1931, when removed to present site and dedicated as the home of the Delaware Academy of Medicine, 1932.

Lovering Avenue and Union Street, in triangle formed by Park Drive, Wilmington. [Bronze Tablet].

DELAWARE CITY SCHOOL #118C

In 1919 Delaware radically altered its state school system, opening a new era in the education of African-American youth. Progress was stimulated by the efforts of the Delaware School Auxiliary Association and its primary supporter, P. S. du Pont, who conducted a statewide effort to replace outdated and overcrowded facilities. On March 9, 1922, the State received the deed for a new building to replace a school located in the Polktown section of the community. The facility housed grades 1 through 8. Citizens expressed their gratitude to Mr. du Pont for his "most generous and valuable gift." The school was closed in 1961. In 1962 the property was sold to the Delaware City Community Park District.

Dragon Run Road, 1/4 mile from intersection with DE 9, Delaware City. (NC 97)

 DUNCAN BEARD

Delaware lock-maker of great distinction and silversmith lived and labored here for about thirty years until his death in 1797. Was a prominent member of Old Drawyers Presbyterian Church. Made contract with State of Delaware in 1776 for manufacture of gun locks.

DE 299, 1.4 miles south east from US 13, Odessa. (NC 72)

 DUPONT POWDER MILLS

On the banks of the Brandywine, one-half mile northeast of this crossroad, Eleuthere Irenee du Pont de Nemours built in 1802 the first DuPont Powder Mills in America. Powder was manufactured there for the United States Government in War of 1812, Mexican War, Civil War, Spanish- American War and Great War. Old mills abandoned 1921.

DE 141, north side, 0.2 miles west of DE 100 and DE 141. (NC 60)

EASTBURN-JEANES MINING COMPLEX
[c. 1816-1900's]

This is the site of the Eastburn-Jeanes farms and mining industry. Marble from the Cockeysville Formation, found in three quarries in the area, was heated in kilns to produce

The **Holy Trinity (Old Swede's) Church** was built in 1698 as a Swedish Lutheran Church. The church was a community center long after Sweden lost its New World claims. Later, in 1791, the church became Protestant Episcopal. (See marker 80, page 49)

quicklime for fertilizer and mortar. The lime was transported over Limestone Road to nearby Pennsylvania, Maryland and southern Delaware. The remaining historic structures include nearby kilns, residences, shops, springhouses, and the ruin of the stone Eastburn barn.

Upper Pike Creek Road (Rd. 295), about 1/4 mile south-west from DE 72 and DE 7. (NC 83)

33   EBENEZER UNITED METHODIST CHURCH

The first meetings of this congregation were held in the homes of its members. In 1824 a stone church building was erected at this location. The growth of the congregation resulted in the replacement of the original building by a one-story frame structure in 1859. Formerly a part of the Hockessin Charge, Ebenezer became a separate station in 1897. A parsonage was constructed soon thereafter. It would serve as home for the church's ministers until it was dismantled in 1968.

With the spread of suburban settlement during the decade of the 1950's, the congregation began to outgrow its facilities once again. Additional property was purchased in 1954, and a new Education Building was completed in 1964. Continued growth resulted in the construction of the present sanctuary in 1975-76. A Christian Life Center was subsequently completed in 1993. For a time the old frame church was utilized for Sunday School classes, and as a meeting place for the local Korean United Methodist congregation. After many years of service to the church and community, the building was demolished in 1998.

North of Newark on the west side of Rd. 324, 3/4 mile south of Rd. 324 and DE 72. (NC 104)

34   EBRIGHT AZIMUTH

The highest benchmark monument in Delaware is located on Ebright Road. This horizontal control mark denotes an elevation of 447.85 feet above sea level. The Delaware Geological Survey through its relationship with the National Geodetic Survey has determined that this benchmark monument is in the vicinity of the highest natural elevation in the state.

Ebright Road, just beyond Concord High School, off Naaman's Road [DE 92]. (NC 85)

35   EDEN PARK 10
[Formerly Monckton Park]

One time home of Robert Morris, signer of Declaration of Independence and financier of American Revolution, who purchased this property in 1783. Bought in 1805 by Peter Bauduy, architect of Old Town Hall, Wilmington. Eden Park Powder Mills established by Garesche 1801.

South Wilmington, east on Fourth Street, cross bridge over Christiana River, and along New Castle Avenue-0.8 mile from bridge. (NC 10M)

36   EDMUND CANTWELL

Near this spot was the home of Edmund Cantwell, first sheriff of New Castle County 1672. Surveyor of many early grants. Here John Moll and Ephraim Herman, deputies of William Penn, met October 28, 1682, taking possession of the Lower Counties, now Kent and Sussex, by Act of Seisin, receiving "turf and twig water and soyle in part of all."

US 13, east side, one mile south of Odessa. Drive east 1.5 miles, turn north - first house. (NC 19M)

37   ENCAMPMENT OF CONTINENTAL TROOPS 1777

Delaware and Maryland regiments, consisting of 1500 men, under command of General William Smallwood, upon order of General Washington, encamped in this vicinity December 21, 1777, to prevent occupation by the British and to protect American interests. Smallwood remained here several months.

Lovering Avenue, north side, in block west of Broom Street, Wilmington. (NC 7M)

LOG CABIN, FORT CHRISTINA PARK

FORT CHRISTINA MONUMENT

FORT CHRISTINA MONUMENT

FORT CHRISTINA PARK

Fort Christina commemorates the landing at "The Rocks" by the first Swedish settlers in 1638 at what is now Wilmington. The monument in the park was a gift from the people of Sweden to the people of the United States. The log cabin in the park is representative of a type of dwelling introduced into this country by the early Swedish settlers. (See makers 39 and 59, pages 35 and 43)

FIRST PRESBYTERIAN CHURCH

This church originally stood at the corner of 10th and Market Streets and was the first Presbyterian church in the city. It was constructed in 1740, just after Wilmington received its charter from King George II. Following the Battle of Brandywine on September 11, 1777, the British used the building as a hospital. After the congregation moved to a larger church in 1878, the Delaware Historical Society used the building until 1916. The church was then moved to this site in Brandywine Park to allow for construction of the Wilmington Library. The building is now operated by the Society of Colonial Dames of America in Delaware, serving as a reminder of Wilmington's role during the American Revolution.

South Park Drive and West Street, Wilmington. (NC 77)

 FORT CHRISTINA

This park commemorates New Sweden, the colony founded when Peter Minuit's expedition landed from the Swedish ships *Kalmar Nyckel* and *Vogel Grip* on the natural wharf of rocks at the riverside about March 29, 1638. Fort Christina, built here, became the first permanent European settlement in the Delaware valley.

Fort Christina Monument was dedicated here June 27, 1938, celebrating the Tercentenary of the landing. Participants included the Swedish Royal Commission led by their Royal Highnesses, The Crown Prince, The Crown Princess, and Prince Bertil, the Finnish Official Delegation, President Franklin D. Roosevelt and Governor Richard C. McMullen of Delaware.

The park was created by the State of Delaware for the Tercentenary in 1938. It was designated a National Historic Landmark by the U. S. Department of Interior March 29, 1963, in the presence of Prince Bertil of Sweden, Vice President Lyndon B. Johnson and other distinguished guests at the celebration of the 325th anniversary of the landing here at "The Rocks."

The monument is a gift of The People of Sweden to The People of the United States. Its entire cost was met by about 225,000 individual subscriptions from residents of almost every community in Sweden responding to a broadcast suggestion. It is a permanent symbol of the friendship between the two peoples.

The monument, designed and executed by the Swedish-American sculptor, Carl Milles, is an irregular hexagon of black Swedish granite. Bas reliefs show contacts between settlers and Indians, Queen Christina on horseback, Governor Johan Printz, the Swedes receiving William Penn, and other scenes. Surmounting the shaft is a stylized wave bearing the *Kalmar Nyckel*.

Fort Christina Park, Wilmington. (Five Plaques on Walls)

40 GIBRALTAR

In 1844, John Rodney Brinkle, grandnephew of Delaware patriot Caesar Rodney, built the Italianate core of this Brandywine granite home, named for the high, prominent rocky outcropping upon which it sits. In 1909, Hugh Rodney Sharp and his wife Isabella Mathieu du Pont Sharp purchased and greatly expanded Gibraltar.

Marian Cruger Coffin, a pioneering woman in the field of landscape architecture, designed the formal gardens on the property and oversaw their installation in the late 1910's and early 1920's. She was responsible for many other well known gardens and designed landscapes throughout the East Coast, including the nearby gardens of Winterthur, Mt. Cuba, and University of Delaware.

Hugh Rodney Sharp was Delaware's preeminent preservationist, restoring the Historic Houses of Odessa, Old Town Hall, the Academy of Medicine, and many others. His

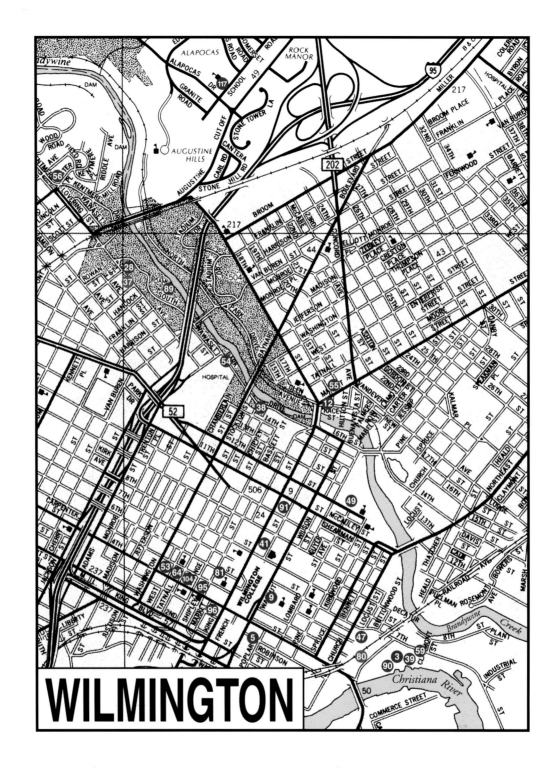

WILMINGTON

Wilmington is halfway between New York City and Washington, D. C., and is a medium sized metropolis that blends the intense activities of the business world with the relaxing cultural and historic events of the area.

extensive philanthropy benefited many local cultural and educational institutions, particularly the University of Delaware. In 1998, Gibraltar was placed on the National Register of Historic Places.

Northwest corner of Pennsylvania and Greenhill Avenues, Wilmington. (NC 108)

41 **GRAVE SITE OF BISHOP PETER SPENCER [1779-1843] AND HIS DEVOTED WIFE, ANNES**

Born a slave, Bishop Spencer was the father of Delaware's independent Black church movement. In 1813, he founded the Union Church of Africans, presently known as the African Union Methodist Protestant Church. The mother AUMP Church stood on this site from 1813 to 1970. The Union American Methodist Episcopal Church [UAME], formally organized in 1865, traces its origins to Spencer. He was also the founder of "August Quarterly" in 1813, one of the oldest Black folk festivals in America.

The Plaza, off French Street, Wilmington. (NC 84)

42 **THE GREEN OR MARKET PLAINE**

Laid out by Petrus Stuyvesant, Dutch Governor, 1655. On this Green stood the old jail and gallows. Here were held the great fairs and weekly markets from early times.

Third and Delaware Streets, corner of the Green, New Castle. (NC 28)

43 **GUNNING BEDFORD HOUSE**

Built about 1760. Home of Gunning Bedford, eleventh Governor of Delaware. Born 1742. Lieutenant-colonel in Haslet's Delaware Regiment. Wounded in Battle of White Plains 1776. Presidential elector 1788. Also home of Caleb P. Bennett, twenty-ninth Governor of Delaware. Born 1758. Served in Haslet's and Hall's Delaware Regiments. With Washington at Yorktown. Commanded forces at New Castle 1812. Great-grandson of Daniel Boone. Later residence

of Andrew C. Gray. Birthplace of George Gray, lawyer, statesman and judge.

The Strand, west side, near Delaware Street, New Castle. [Bronze Tablet]

44 **GUNNING BEDFORD, JR.**

1747-1812. Member of Continental Congress and of Annapolis Convention. A framer of United States Constitution, which Delaware was first to ratify. Appointed first District Judge of Delaware by President Washington. Purchased this property 1793 as country home, naming it "Lombardy." Buried at Tenth and Market Streets, Wilmington. Reinterred 1921 at Masonic Home.

US 202, north side, 0.3 mile west of Foulk Road [DE 261], at driveway to house. (NC 6)

45 **HALE-BYRNES HOUSE**
-Stanton, Delaware-

George Washington's "General Staff Headquarters" on September 6, 1777. Here Generals Washington, Lafayette, Wayne, Maxwell, Sullivan and Greene planned defense of Wilmington. House built circa 1750 by Samuel Hale. Owner 1776 ~ Daniel Byrnes ~ a miller and preacher. Restored by Delaware Society for Preservation of Antiquities. Donated to state in 1971.

DE 7, at Ogletown Road [DE 4], 5.5 miles from Wilmington. (NC 50)

46 **HISTORIC MUSEUM**

Rear of house built in seventeenth century. Main building built after 1738 by Doctor John Finney. Home of Nicholas Van Dyke, seventh Governor of Delaware. The marriage of Ann Van Dyke to Kensey Johns, Sr., took place here April 24, 1784. George Washington was a guest at this wedding.

Delaware and Fourth Streets, north-west corner, New Castle. [Bronze Tablet]

NEMOURS MANSION AND GARDENS

NEMOURS MANSION AND GARDENS

INTERIOR, NEMOURS MANSION

Nemours Mansion and Gardens - Nemours, site of the du Pont ancestral home in North Central France, was chosen by Alfred I. du Pont as the name for his beautiful 300-acre country estate north of Wilmington.

HOLY TRINITY CHURCH
[Heliga Trefaldighets Kyrka]

In 1638 a colony from Sweden landed at "The Rocks" nearby. There they built Fort Christina, worshipped therein until 1667, and then built a log church at Cranehook on south side of Christiana River. In 1698, inspired by their pastor, Eric Bjork, they erected Holy Trinity Church. The tower was added in 1802.The Church of Sweden withdrew in 1791 and was thenceforth succeeded by the Protestant Episcopal Church.

Seventh and Church Streets, south-east corner, Wilmington. [Bronze Tablet]

 THE HOME OF WILLIAM JULIUS "JUDY" JOHNSON
Born October 26, 1899-Died June 14, 1989

In 1975 William Julius "Judy" Johnson became the first Delawarean elected to the National Baseball Hall of Fame. During his career, 1921 through 1936, Johnson was considered the best third baseman in the Negro Leagues. In 1935, Johnson served as captain of the Pittsburgh Crawfords, a team that also featured Hall of Famers Satchel Paige, Oscar Charleston, Josh Gibson and Cool Papa Bell. Later he served as a scout for the Philadelphia Athletics, the Philadelphia Phillies, and the Milwaukee Braves. This house, where Johnson and his wife Anita lived for 55 years, is listed in the National Register of Historic Places.

Kiamensi Road (Rd. 331) and Newport Gap Pike (DE 62), north of Newport. (NC 95)

 HOWARD HIGH SCHOOL
First Secondary School for Blacks in Delaware

Founded in 1867 by the Association for the Moral Improvement and Education of Colored People and named for Civil War General Oliver Otis Howard, the original school was located at 12th and Orange Streets. Pierre S. du Pont was the major benefactor for the new building, opened in 1928 on this site. With the annexation of the

adjoining Howard Career Center in 1975, Howard's role as the major educational institution for Blacks expanded to include students from the total Delaware community.

North Poplar Street in front of Howard High School, near West 13th Street, Wilmington. (NC 82)

 INDIAN TREATY

Philip Calvert, Governor of Maryland, and Pinna, King of Picthanomicta on Delaware, on behalf of Passagonke Indians, made and signed a treaty of peace and amity at Odessa [then called Appoquinimi] September 19, 1661.

US 13, east side, Odessa. (NC 20M)

 IN MEMORY OF PHILIP AND LYDIA LAIRD

Former owners of the Read House, their home for fifty-five years. They were longtime benefactors of New Castle doing much to encourage and promote the preservation and architectural beauty of this colonial town.

The Strand, between Delaware and Harmony Streets, New Castle. (Tablet on Pole)

 IRON HILL

Indian names, Marettico, meaning hill of hard stone, and Suquasehum, meaning iron. Minqua Indians had a fort on hill which Senecas attacked, 1663. British troops encamped on hill, 1777, and American troops, under Caesar A. Rodney, 1814. Iron discovered prior to 1661. Mined until 1891. Largest ore pit one mile north.

Old Baltimore Pike (Rd. 26), north side, 1.5 miles west of Cooch's Bridge, at intersection of road over summit of Iron Hill. (NC 54M)

 JOHN DICKINSON

Nearby is grave of John Dickinson, lawyer, scholar, and statesman. Member Colonial Assemblies of Delaware and Pennsylvania and Legislative Council of Delaware State.

INTERIOR, NEMOURS MANSION

GARDENS, NEMOURS MANSION

AERIAL, NEMOURS MANSION

The Nemours Mansion, a fine example of a modified Louis XVI French château, was completed in 1910 and contains over one hundred rooms. The gardens are one of the finest examples of French-style gardens in America.

Delegate from Pennsylvania to Stamp Act Congress. Representative in Continental Congress from Pennsylvania and Delaware, and president of both states. Signer for Delaware of Articles of Confederation. Member from Delaware and Chairman Annapolis Convention. Delaware Delegate to Federal Constitutional Convention, and framer and signer of Constitution. Judge Delaware Court of Appeals. President Second Delaware Constitutional Convention. Rendered military service in Revolution. Author of famous "Letters from a Farmer in Pennsylvania." A founder of Dickinson College. Lived in Kent County and at Eighth and Market Streets, Wilmington.

Fourth and Washington Streets, north-east corner, Wilmington. [Bronze Tablet]

54 JOHN McKINLY
President [Governor] of Delaware, 1777

The only known governor born in a foreign country. John McKinly was born in Northern Ireland on February 24, 1721. He immigrated to Wilmington in 1742, began a medical practice, and became actively involved in Delaware politics. McKinly served as a member of the Colonial Assembly, President of the Council of Safety, and helped to establish the Delaware Medical Society. He died on August 31, 1796.

South Park Drive, in Brandywine Cemetery, near intersection with North Adams Street, Wilmington. (NC 81)

55 JOSEPH TATNALL HOUSE

Built about 1760. Anthony Wayne's headquarters 1777. George Washington, Lafayette, Wayne, and other officers met here to hold council and hear reports prior to Battle of Brandywine. Later occupied by British. Joseph Tatnall owned and operated original flour mills on the Brandywine, and supplied flour to Continental Army.

1803 Market Street, west side of US 13, third house south of Nineteenth Street, Wilmington. [Bronze Tablet]

56 KENTMERE PARKWAY

This 14.7 acre strip of land, connecting Rockford Park and Grove with Brandywine Park, was designed by famed American landscape architect Frederick Law Olmstead. The land was donated by two Wilmington businessmen, William M. Fields and William Poole Bancroft, the latter known as the father of the Wilmington park system. Omlstead's design was based on Fields' research of parkways in other eastern cities he visited. He concluded that the right-of-way should be 150 feet wide, with buildings set back 25 feet on either side. Kentmere Parkway was completed to Fields' specifications in 1891.

Brandwine Park, Wilmington. (NC 109)

57 LAFAYETTE `

General Lafayette en route to Virginia, to command expedition against Benedict Arnold, landed 1500 troops here, with cannon, stores, and ammunition, March 2, 1781. Council of Maryland issued warrant to impress carriages, teams, and drivers for his use at Christiana Bridge and vessels, hands, etc., at Head of Elk.

Old Baltimore Pike (DE 7), south at crossroads, at north end of Christiana Bridge, Christiana. (NC 51M)

58 LANDING PLACE OF WILLIAM PENN

Near here October 27,1682, William Penn first stepped on American soil. He proceeded to the fort and performed Livery of Seisin. "He took the key, thereof...we did deliver unto him 1 turf with a twig upon it, a porringer with river water and soyle, in part of all."

The Strand and Delaware Street, north-east corner, New Castle. (NC 25)

BRANDYWINE RIVER AND WILMINGTON

WALKER MILL, BRANDYWINE RIVER

BRANDYWINE RIVER, WILMINGTON

HOTEL DU PONT, WILMINGTON

The **Greater Wilmington Area** offers the fast pace of the business world, the serenity of a walk along the Brandywine River, the exploration of a historical site, and the elegance of the famous Hotel du Pont.

59 **THE LOG CABIN**

The log cabin was unknown to the first English and Dutch settlers. It was introduced into America from Sweden here at Fort Christina. Cheap, quickly and easily built, and snug, it was an ideal pioneer home. It spread to the Pacific with westward settlement. Several different log construction techniques developed later, some were Swedish, some of other origins.

This cabin is the early Swedish type, with rough-hewn round logs saddle-notched at the ends, chinked with sticks, twigs, and grass-mixed clay, It has one large room with a fireplace and a huge shelf above for extra sleeping and storage place. It once stood on land of the early Stalcop family. It was given by Mr. and Mrs. H. C. Fenimore in memory of his mother, Ellen Jane Fenimore, who saved it from destruction early in this century.

Fort Christina Park, Wilmington. (Two Plaques on Wall)

 60 **LONG HOOK**
Home of Major Peter Jaquett, Hero of the Revolution

Named for its location on a prominent curvature of the Christina River, Long Hook was home to several generations of the Jaquett family. The first to settle in this vicinity was Jean Paul Jaquett, a French Protestant who served as Vice Director and Chief Magistrate of New Netherlands on the South River (1655-1657). It was here that Major Peter Jaquett was born on April 6, 1754. A distinguished officer of the Delaware Line in the American Revolution, Major Jaquett was a participant in many of the war's most important campaigns. Twice wounded, he was by the side of both Colonel Haslet at Princeton and Baron De Kalb at Camden when they were mortally wounded.

Following the war Major Jaquett returned to his boyhood home, where he resided until his death in 1834. Many distinguished persons, including George Washington and the Marquis de Lafayette, are said to have visited here.

West side south US 13, one mile south of the US 13 B Christina River Bridge, Wilmington. (NC 103)

 61 **LONG HOOK FARM**

Formerly residence of Major Peter Jaquett, distinguished officer of Delaware Line in Revolution. Born here 1755, died here 1834. Buried at Old Swedes' Church, Wilmington. Land originally owned by Jean Paul Jaquett, Vice Director and Chief Magistrate of New Netherland on the South River, 1655-1657.

US 13, west side, 1.1 miles south of Christiana River. (NC 12M)

 62 **MASON AND DIXON LINE**

The boundary between Delaware and Maryland is part of famous line surveyed 1763-1767 by Charles Mason and Jeremiah Dixon, under agreement between Lord Baltimore and heirs of William Penn. The excavations nearby were made 1804-1805 in first attempt to construct a canal connecting Delaware and Chesapeake Bays.

Old Baltimore Pike (Rd. 26) at DE-MD State Line, north side, 2.8 miles west of Cooch's Bridge. (NC 55M)

63 **MASON AND DIXON'S TANGENT STONE**

In the field between this road and the railroad track is located the famous tangent stone, surveyed and marked by Mason and Dixon in 1764, when surveying the boundary line between Maryland and Delaware. The tangent stone is on the circumference of an arc twelve miles from New Castle.

DE 2 [Lincoln Highway], east side, two miles south-west of Newark, at DE-MD State Line. (NC 38M)

 64 **MEETING HOUSE 1816**
Religious Society of Friends

Grew from Newark Meeting established 1682. Present house is third in this vicinity. Friends School, begun here in 1748, has operated continuously. Among 3,000 buried in yard are founders of Wilmington, John Dickinson, "Penman

Fort Delaware on Pea Patch Island in the Delaware River, was completed in early 1859, with the First Union Army unit occupying the fort in early 1861. In 1862, the first Confederate prisoners arrived. At its peak, after the Battle of Gettysburg, approximately 12,500 Confederate soldiers were detained on the island. Today the fort is a Delaware State Park.

of the Revolution," and Thomas Garrett, leader of Underground Railroad on Delmarva Peninsula.

West and 4th Streets, in Meeting House Yard, Wilmington. (NC 76)

65 MOUNT OLIVE CEMETERY

In 1862 the members of mother AUMP Church, also known as the Union Church of African Members, purchased property at the corner of Lancaster Avenue and Union Street in Wilmington for the purpose of establishing a cemetery. In 1914 the church sold the property, then known as St. Peter's Cemetery, for the construction of Bancroft Parkway. Remains were disinterred and reburied at Mount Olive. Many prominent citizens and community leaders are buried here. In 1980 the Friends of Mount Olive Cemetery was established to provide ongoing care and maintenance.

DE 48-DE 100 at the intersection with DE 100-DE 141. (NC 87)

66 NAAMAN'S BRIDGE

First bridge built 1682. Used by Swedes, Dutch, and English before the coming of Penn, being road from Fort Casimir [now New Castle] to Upland [now Chester] and Tinicum. Second bridge built 1800. Toll bridge until 1832.

US 13, west side, 0.5 miles south of DE-PA State Line. (NC 4M)

67 NAAMAN'S CREEK

Named for Indian chief, 1655. Chief Peminacka of Minqua Tribe deeded large tract of land along Naaman's Creek to John Risingh, Governor, New Sweden. Noted Swedish artists, Gustavus Hesslius and Adolph Ulric Wertmuller, lived on plantations on this creek.

US 13, west side, at creek and 100 feet south of Block House, DE-PA State Line. (NC 3)

68 NEWARK ACADEMY

Founded at New London, Pennsylvania in 1741 by Rev. Dr. Francis Alison. Removed in 1752 to Cecil County, Maryland, and in 1767 to Newark. Chartered by Thomas and Richard Penn 1769. Closed from 1777 to 1780 on account of RevoluionaryWar. Merged with Newark College [now University of Delaware] 1834. Separated from College 1869 and continued as independent Academy until 1898. Many famous men were educated in this school.

Main [DE 273] and Academy Streets, south-east corner, Newark. (NC 35)

69 NEWARK UNION

Successor to Newark Monthly Meeting of Friends. Established about 1682. Early meetings held at Morgan Dewit's and at Valentine Hollingsworth's. Named from plantation called New Wark or New Worke patented to Hollingsworth, who in 1687 donated one-half acre for a burying place, "being some already buryed in ye spot."

Daynard Boulevard at Newark Union Road. (NC 5)

70 NEW CASTLE

Colonial capital until 1777. Indian village Tamakonck, place of beaver. First town laid out in Delaware. Dutch "Fort Casimir" 1651. Swedish "Fort Trafaldigheets" 1654. Dutch "New Amstel" 1655. English "New Castle" 1664. Home of three signers of the Declaration, George Read, George Ross, and Thomas McKean.

o *Corner of Washington Avenue and River Road, west side of highway, 0.7 miles from Court House Square, New Castle. (NC 30M)*

o *Northern entrance of town of New Castle. (NC 21M)*

o *Washington Avenue and Hare's Corner Road [DE 273], south side, one mile from Court House Square, New Castle. (NC 31M)*

INTERIOR, WINTERTHUR

INTERIOR, WINTERTHUR

INTERIOR, WINTERTHUR

INTERIOR, WINTERTHUR

Winterthur is the former country estate of Henry Francis du Pont, a great-grandson of the founder of the DuPont Company. The estate is now a museum whose attractions reflect the two passions of Henry's life; horticulture and antiques. The mansion is a showcase for antiques and American decorative arts.

NEW CASTLE AND FRENCHTOWN RAILROAD

Built 1832. One of the first railroads in country. Extended from this point to Frenchtown on the Elk River. Important connecting link between the North and South. Absorbed by Delaware Railroad 1856.

- o *South end of Strand, New Castle. (NC 26)*
- o *River Road and Washington Avenue, east side, New Castle. (NC 29M)*
- o *DE 896, east side, one mile south of Glasgow. (NC 44M)*

 NEW CASTLE COMMON

This land is part of a tract of one thousand acres set apart by William Penn in 1701 for the inhabitants of the town of New Castle. Trustees were appointed and incorporated by Penn's heirs in 1764, whose successors still hold and manage the land.

- o *Dalby Park, New Castle. (NC 13)*
- o *US 13, east side, six miles south of Wilmington, at Hare's corner (DE 273). (NC 14M)*

 NEW CASTLE UNITED METHODIST CHURCH

The origin of Methodism in this community can be traced to the years prior to the American Revolution, when pioneering clergymen such as Thomas Webb and Francis Asbury visited here to spread the message of their faith. Due to the predominance of long-established denominations, and a relatively small membership, early attempts to establish a Methodist society were unsuccessful. After a long period of inactivity, efforts were revived, and by 1819 a group was organized and meeting regularly in the homes of its members.

Desiring a permanent place of worship, the congregation purchased a parcel of land from Richard Sexton on September 28, 1820. A small brick chapel was erected on the site, which is now contained within the adjoining graveyard. Then known as Nazareth Methodist Episcopal Church, it

served the congregation until 1863, when the present church was built. A major expansion was undertaken in 1876, with the construction of a Sunday School addition at the rear of the church. Facilities were further expanded with the completion of the present Fellowship Hall in 1956.

510 Delaware Street, New Castle. (NC 111)

 ODESSA

Indian village Appoquinimi. Part of large grant to Alexander D'Hinoyossa, Vice-Director of New Amstel. Edmund Cantwell, second owner of tract 1673. Village named Cantwell's Bridge 1731. Once important grain shipping center. Named Odessa, 1855, after Russian grain port.

Main Street, between US 13 North and South, Odessa. (NC 18)

 OLD CLAYMONT HIGH SCHOOL

Constructed 1924-25. Also known as the Green Street School. Prominent in United States history as the first public high school in the 17 segregated states to be legally integrated.

In January 1951, eight black students applied for admission. Due to the "separate but equal" education system in place at that time, the Claymont Board of Education was unable to permit their entry. In July 1951, noted civil rights attorney Louis L. Redding of Wilmington filed a civil action suit seeking the students' admission. On April 1, 1952, Delaware Chancellor Collins J. Seitz rendered his landmark decision, declaring that opportunities for black students in local schools were not equal to those of whites, and that the situation should be remedied immediately. This decision was upheld by the Delaware Supreme Court. On September 3, 1952, the Claymont Board voted to admit twelve students, who with their parents, the Board, and Redding, swiftly made legal preparation for their admission September 4. When school administrators were ordered September 5 by the State Board

REFLECTING POOL, WINTERTHUR

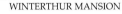
WINTERTHUR MANSION

GARDENS, WINTERTHUR

GROUNDS, WINTERTHUR

Winterthur - One of Henry du Pont's passions was horticulture. Around 1906, Henry took over supervision of Winterthur grounds. Today, the naturalistic gardens feature native and exotic plants, ponds, woods and meadowland on the almost 1,000 acre estate. Year round events include Point-to-Point Steeplechase Races and the Yuletide Tour.

of Education and Delaware Attorney General to send the students home to await a U.S. Supreme Court ruling, Claymont Superintendent H. E. Stahl and the local Board refused, successfully insisting that the students stay enrolled. Mrs. Pauline Dyson, a long-time teacher of Claymont's black students, worked closely with school district officials and the community to ensure success of the effort. The Delaware case was later included for argument in the famous *Brown vs. Board of Education* suit. Claymont's first integrated class graduated in 1954.

High school classes were moved to another facility in 1969. Middle school classes were located here until 1978. In 1980 the building became the home of the Claymont Community Center.

Green Street, west side, near the intersection with Lawson Street, Claymont (NC 99).

 OLD COLLEGE
Erected 1833-1834

This building contained a chapel [called the Oratory], class, dormitory, dining, administrative, and student society rooms. New Ark College, chartered February 5, 1833, opened its doors for instruction May 8, 1834. Name changed to Delaware College, April 4, 1843. Willard Hall, first president of board of trustees; Rev. Dr. Eliphalet W. Gilbert, first president; Nathan Monroe and John Holmes Agnew, first professors. Alexander T. Gray, the first student, was enrolled as a sophomore.

Main Street, north side, on campus of University of Delaware, Newark. [Bronze Tablet]

77 **OLD DRAWYERS**

Presbyterian Church organized about 1700. Original name Appoquinimy. Site purchased and first church erected 1711. Assisted in formation of Presbytery of New Castle 1717. Present church erected 1773. Many founders of the state are buried here.

US 13, center of dual highway, north of Odessa. (NC 17M)

 OLD FEEDER CANAL

Excavations begun May 2, 1804, in first attempt to build a canal between Chesapeake and Delaware Bays. Feeder was intended to conduct water from Elk Creek to a ship canal to extend from Welsh Point on Elk to Mendenhall's Landing on Christiana. Work abandoned 1805.

US 40, ten miles west of US 13 and 1.5 miles west of Glasgow. (NC 59M)

79 **OLD ST. ANNE'S P. E. CHURCH**

As early as 1705 a log chapel was established at "Appoquinimy" by the S.P.G. with the Rev. Thomas Jenkins appointed its first missionary in 1708. Queen Anne of England, for whom the church was named, is said to have been a patron. This church was built 1765-1771 through efforts of the Rev. Philip Reading, buried here in 1778.

DE 71, west side, near Rd. 447, 0.4 mile south of Middletown. (NC 74)

80 **OLD SWEDE'S CHURCH**

Erected by Swedish settlers 1698.
Located on the Pennsylvania Railroad elevated tracks between 6th and 7th Streets, Wilmington. (NC 8M)

 OLD TOWN HALL

Built 1798. Part of site donated by John Dickinson. Architect, Peter Bauduy. Procession formed here in 1799 to commemorate death of Washington. Election of Jefferson in 1801 celebrated by public banquet. During War of 1812, town meetings arranged for the defense of the borough. Dinner given Lafayette, 1824. Mexican War victories

ORIGINAL GARDEN, DUPONT FAMILY HOME

ELEUTHERIAN MILLS, DUPONT HOUSE

HAGLEY MUSEUM, MACHINE SHOP

FRENCH GARDEN, DUPONT FAMILY HOME

The **Hagley Museum** is located along the Brandywine River on the site of the first DuPont black powder works. The museum provides a unique glimpse into American life at home and at work in the nineteenth century. The du Pont family home, Eleutherian Mills, was built in 1803 and is furnished with antiques and memorabilia of five generations of du Pont's associated with the home. (See marker 31, page 31)

celebrated, 1847. Henry Clay's body lay in state here, 1852. Volunteers recruited by Union Army, 1861-1865. Purchased from the city by Historical Society of Delaware, 1917. Red Cross Headquarters during Great War. Restored by Old Town Hall Association, 1927.

Market Street, east side, second building south of Sixth Street, Wilmington. [Bronze Tablet].

 82 **OLIVER EVANS**
(1755-1819) Inventor and Engineer

Born in Newport, Delaware, September 13, 1755, son of Charles and Ann Stalcop Evans. Invented automatic machinery for flour mills; first high-pressure steam engine adapted to commercial use in America; and first American land vehicle to move under steam power. Died in New York City April 15, 1819.

Augustine Avenue and Market Street, Newport. (NC 71)

83 **PACKET ALLEY**

Packet boats from Philadelphia met stage coaches here for Frenchtown, Maryland, chief line of communication from north to Baltimore and south. Andrew Jackson, David Crockett, Daniel Webster, Henry Clay, Lord Ashburton, Sam Houston, Louis Napoleon, Stonewall Jackson, Indians [led by Osceola and Black Hawk] en route to visit "Great Father" in Washington---all passed this way.

The Strand and Packet Alley, east side, between Delaware and Harmony Streets, New Castle. (NC 24)

84 **PENCADER CHURCH**

Organized by Welsh Presbyterians prior to 1710. First called Welsh Tract Church. Name soon changed to Pencader, a Welsh term meaning "chief chair or seat." British sick and wounded were brought to the church after Battle of Cooch's Bridge, September 3, 1777.

US 40, seven miles west from US 13, north side, Glasgow. (NC 58M)

85 **PRESBYTERIAN CHURCH**

Founded as a Dutch Reformed Church, 1657. The first building was on the Strand end of the church lot. This church was one of 7 which organized the first Presbytery in America in 1706. The present brick meeting house was built 1707.

Second Street, east side, between Delaware and Harmony Streets, New Castle. (NC 75)

 86 **THE RIVER ROAD**

Portion of the early cart road laid out by Augustine Herrman, Lord of Bohemia Manor, to connect his Maryland estate with Appoquinimink Creek and the town of New Castle. Known as "The Old Man's Road," this was one of the earliest links between the Delaware River and the Chesapeake Bay.

Fifth and South Streets, south-east corner, New Castle. (NC 73)

87 **ROBERT KIRKWOOD**

Born 1756 on farm adjoining this church. Senior captain of Delaware Battalion of Continental Army after Battle of Camden, S. C., 1780. Distinguished throughout Revolution for undaunted bravery and devotion to cause of liberty. Brevetted major 1783. Killed in battle with Indians 1791 near Fort Recovery, Ohio, his thirty-third engagement.

DE 2 [Lincoln Highway], north side, adjoining cemetery,White Clay Creek Church, eleven miles west of Wilmington. (NC 34M)

 88 **ROBINSON HOUSE**

Built about 1723, on land patented by Governor Andros to Swedes and Dutch in 1675. Acquired by Thomas Robinson 1749. Robinson killed in Indian warfare in 1766. Washington, Anthony Wayne, Lafayette, and "Light Horse"

ROCKFORD TOWER, WILMINGTON

GIBRALTAR, WILMINGTON

BRANDYWINE RIVER, WILMINGTON

GARDENS, GIBRALTAR, WILMINGTON

Rockford Tower, completed in 1902, is a water storage tank and observatory constructed of natural fieldstone and is located in the Brandywine State Park. (See marker 89, page 53) The **Brandywine River** flows through the eastern edge of downtown Wilmington. **Gibraltar** is a magnificent Brandywine granite home with formal gardens designed by a noted landscape architect. (See marker 40, page 35)

Harry Lee were guests here. Across road Jasper Yeates established flour mill which operated two centuries.

US 13, a few feet south of Block House on road at right is the Robinson House, now known as Naaman's Tea House. (NC 2M)

89 **ROCKFORD TOWER**

In 1895, Theodore Leisen, engineer for the Wilmington Board of Park Commissioners, recommended that "a large pavilion and observatory" be built in Rockford Park on what was called Mt. Salem Hill, the highest point in the city at 330 feet above sea level. His proposal coincided with the Board of Water Commissioners' conclusion that Wilmington was in need of a new water tower in that neighborhood. The two boards merged their projects in Rockford Tower. Built between 1899 and 1902, the half-million-gallon water storage tank and observatory is constructed of natural field stone and is an example of the Italian Renaissance Revival style. Rockford Tower is 57 feet in diameter at the base, 75 feet high to the floor of the observatory, and reaches a total height of 115 feet.

Brandywine State Park, Wilmington. (NC 110)

90 **THE ROCKS**

First landing place of the Swedes, 1638. Site of Fort Christina.

Bank of the Christiana River, north-east of the landing place at Fourth Street Wharf, Wilmington. (NC 9M)

91 **SAINT JOSEPH CHURCH**

The cradle of African-American Catholicism in Delaware, St. Joseph Church was organized in 1889 by Father John A. DeRuyter of the Josephites. Services were first held in the basement of St. Mary's Church on 6th and Pine Streets. Incorporated as St. Joseph's Society for Colored Missions on March 4, 1890, the first church structure was dedicated in October of the same year. During the next few years, Father DeRuyter expanded the church's role in the community to include an orphanage, a school and a free dispensary. One of the school's most prominent students was State Senator Herman M. Holloway, Sr., the first African-American to serve in the Delaware State Senate.

1012 French Street, Wilmington. (NC 94)

92 **SAINT MARY'S CHURCH**

Site of first Catholic church in Delaware, usually called "Coffee Run" Church. Land purchased 1772 by Rev. Matthias Manners. First church erected shortly thereafter. Last church, erected by Rev. Patrick Kenny, remained standing until 1908. Services discontinued in 1884 upon erection of churches at Hockessin and Ashland.

Lancaster Pike [DE 48], 4.7 miles from Union Street, Wilmington. (NC 32)

93 **SAMUEL DAVIES**

Born here 1723. Noted Welsh minister and educator. Secured recognition of Presbyterian Church in Virginia. Predicted career for Washington whom he termed "that heroic youth." Raised funds in England and Scotland for Nassau Hall, now Princeton. Elected President of Princeton, 1758. Died 1761. House was quarters of British General Grey, September 2, 1777.

DE 71 to Kirkwood, west side, one mile north-east of Summit Bridge. (NC 46M)

94 **SAMUEL PATTERSON**

Operated flour mill one-fourth mile south. Was captain in French and Indian War. In American Revolution was member of Boston Relief Committee, colonel of Delaware battalion of famous "Flying Camp," Brigadier General of Delaware militia and first Treasurer of Delaware State. Died 1785.

THE VILLAGE OF ARDEN

OLD TOWN HALL MUSEUM, WILMINGTON

ROCKWOOD ESTATE, WILMINGTON

THE GRAND OPERA HOUSE, WILMINGTON

The **Village of Arden** was founded in 1900 by artists and craftspeople as Delaware's only single-tax community. Almost half of the village is in greens, roads, paths and buffering forests. (See marker 107, page 59) **Rockwood** is an extraordinary example of mid-19th Rural Gothic architecture, unique to Delaware. It is located on Shipley Road, Wilmington. The **Old Town Hall Museum** is a Georgian-style building that functioned as a center of city government and social activities through the early 20th century. The **Grand Opera House** is Delaware's Center for the Performing Arts. The restored 1871 theater has an unusual cast-iron façade.

Buried in Presbyterian Cemetery at Christiana.

Old Baltimore Pike (Rd.336), south side, 0.6 mile west of Christiana, at intersection of road leading to Smalley's Dam. (NC 52M)

95 SHIPLEY HOUSE

Site of mansion house built 1735 by William Shipley, virtual founder of Wilmington, upon tract of land extending from Market to West and from Second to Fifth Streets. It stood 148 years. Tradition says he located here because of a remarkable dream by his wife, Elizabeth.

Fourth and Shipley Streets, south-west corner, Wilmington. [Bronze Tablet]

96 SIGN OF THE SHIP TAVERN

Site of famous tavern of Revolutionary days, known as "The Sign of the Ship." John Marshall was then inn-keeper. Officers of Continental Army were quartered here. Washington, Lafayette, Aaron Burr and Commodore Perry were among its distinguished guests. Captain Patrick O'Flinn, officer of American Revolution, was proprietor, 1797-1818.

Third and Market Streets, south-east corner, Wilmington. [Bronze Tablet]

97 SITE OF CRANE HOOK CHURCH

Near this spot was established the third place of worship in Delaware. Built 1667 by Swedes and Dutch. Both held services here for thirty-two years. After the building of "Old Swedes" Church in Wilmington in 1698, the church was abandoned.

Drive along New Castle Avenue, south Wilmington, two miles from Christiana Bridge to Lambson Lane. Crane Hook Church stood about 1.5 miles north-east of junction. (NC 11M)

98 SITE OF FORT CASIMIR

One hundred feet to the east of this point is site of Fort Casimir. Erected by Dutch 1651. Taken by Swedes 1654, called Fort Trefaldigheets or Trinity. Retaken by Dutch under Petrus Stuyvesant in person September 11, 1655.

Second and Chestnut Streets, south-east corner, New Castle. (NC 23)

99 SITE OF HOME OF GEORGE READ

Born September 18, 1733, died September 21, 1798. Member of the Congress of the Revolution, the convention that framed the Constitution of the United States, and of the first Congress under it; Judge of Admiralty, President and Chief Justice of Delaware, and signer of the Declaration of Independence. House destroyed by fire, April, 1824.

The Strand, west side, between Delaware and Harmony Streets, New Castle. [Bronze Tablet]

100 SOUTH WILMINGTON
Cradle of African-American Political Leadership

William J. Winchester, after serving 16 years on Wilmington City Council, became the first of his race elected to the Delaware House of Representatives. He served from 1948 until his death in 1952. Herman M. Holloway, Sr., became the first African-American elected to the State Senate in 1964. Henrietta Johnson was the first African-American female elected to the House of Representatives, serving from 1970-1978.

New Castle Avenue and South Claymont Street, Wilmington. (NC 86)

CORBIT-SHARP HOUSE, ODESSA

APPOQUINIMINK FRIENDS MEETING HOUSE, ODESSA

BRICK HOTEL GALLERY, ODESSA

GARDEN, CORBIT-SHARP HOUSE, ODESSA

Odessa, known in the 18th century as Cantwell's Bridge, played a vital role in commercial life along the Delaware River as a busy grain and shipping port. Today you can stroll down tree-lined streets and admire examples of 18th and 19th-century architecture including Winterthur's four Historic Homes of Odessa. (See marker 74, page 47 and marker 4, page 21)

SWANWYCK

Swedish settlement established in this vicinity 1654 under Governor Johan Risuingh. Foot dyke across marshes connected New Amstel [New Castle] with land of Hans Block, early Dutch settler residing near here.

New Castle Ferry Yard. (NC 70)

 TALBOT'S FORT

Colonel George Talbot, cousin of Lord Baltimore, in defiance of William Penn's claim to Delaware, erected a fort nearby, 1684, on land of the widow Ogle. Talbot dispossessed settlers between here and Iron Hill who refused to acknowledge Baltimore as proprietor. Fort garrisoned about two years. Boundary settled by agreement, 1760; surveyed by Mason and Dixon, 1763; confirmed by proclamation of the Provincial Governor John Penn, 1775.

Old Baltimore Pike (Rd. 336), drive west at cross roads in Christiana 0.5 mile, tablet on boulder on north side of road to Newark. [Bronze Tablet]

103 **TAYLOR'S BRIDGE SCHOOL**
[District No. 66]

On April 5, 1923, a frame schoolhouse located nearby was destroyed by a storm. Within two weeks the General Assembly appropriated $5,000 to construct a new school. Although the amount proved to be inadequate, P. S. du Pont, through the Delaware School Auxiliary Association, provided the balance necessary to complete the project. On October 27, 1923, the State of Delaware purchased three acres on this site to build the new brick one-room structure. Construction began shortly thereafter. In 1949 the school closed and the district was consolidated with the Smyrna School District. On April 21, 1950, the Taylor's Bridge Community Center, Inc., purchased the property for one dollar and transformed the structure into a community center.

DE 9, east side, Taylor's Bridge. (NC 93)

 THOMAS GARRETT
Stationmaster on the Underground Railroad

Born August 21, 1789, in Upper Darby, Pennsylvania. Garrett came to Wilmington in 1822. A prominent merchant, his home and business were located nearby on Shipley Street. Garrett was committed to the anti-slavery efforts of his Quaker faith. He is credited with assisting more than 2,700 of "God's Poor" to escape slavery through the secret network known as the Underground Railroad. Though he was convicted and fined by the U.S. District Court in 1848 for aiding runaway slaves, he refused to abandon the fight to abolish slavery. After his death on January 25, 1871, Black Wilmingtonians carried him to the Quaker Cemetery at 4th and West Streets in appreciation of his unwavering commitment to the emancipation of slaves.

Shipley and 4th Streets, Wilmington. (NC 88)

 TOWN HALL AND MARKET HOUSE

Built 1823. Meeting place of Federal Courts. Many important town meetings held here. Fire-engine house in early days.

Second Street, west side, near Delaware Street, New Castle. (NC 27)

 VAN DYKE HOUSE

Built about 1820 by Senator Nicholas Van Dyke. The marriage of Dorcas Van Dyke to Charles I. du Pont took place here October 6, 1824. At this wedding the Marquis de la Fayette was a guest, and gave the bride in marriage.

Delaware and Third Streets, south-west corner, New Castle. [Bronze Tablet]

UNIVERSITY OF DELAWARE, NEWARK

C & D CANAL, LOOKING EAST

UNIVERSITY OF DELAWARE, NEWARK

C & D CANAL, ENTRANCE AT DELAWARE RIVER

The **University of Delaware** in Newark traces its roots to Delaware College (originally New Ark College, the first college in the state, chartered in 1833) and the adjacent Women's College (chartered in 1914). The two officially became the University of Delaware in 1921. (See marker 68, page 45 and marker 76, page 49) **Chesapeake and Delaware Canal** was opened for business in 1829, after years of planning and construction. Today the canal is a modern sea level, electronically controlled commercial waterway, and one of the world's busiest. The canal is listed on the National Register of Historic Places.

THE VILLAGE OF ARDEN

Arden is an intentional community, founded in 1900 by social reformers Frank Stephens, a sculptor, and Will Price, an architect, to create a society based on Henry George's single tax economics and William Morris's arts and craft philosophy. Incorporated in 1967, the village continues to be governed by these taxation and community ideals. All residential land is held in a trust. Leaseholders own their homes and pay property tax [land rent] determined by elected assessors. Town meetings reflect an enduring model of direct democracy. Almost half of the 162 acres is in greens, roads, paths and buffering forests. Arts and crafts continue to flourish in Arden.

2126 The Highway, front of Town Hall, Arden. (NC 92)

 WASHINGTON DINED HERE

This house during Revolution was known as Buck or Carson's Tavern. George Washington stopped here several times. His diary September 3, 1774, states: "dined at Buck Tavern [Carsons] and lodg'd at Newcastle." The Hessian general, Knyphausen, had headquarters here September 2, 1777.

DE 896, west side, south of canal. (NC 45M)

 WASHINGTON'S EARTHWORKS

The American Army numbering about 11,000 encamped between Red Clay Creek and Newport September 6 to 9, 1777. Earthworks constructed for the protection of the camp are plainly visible on the edge of the hill overlooking the creek.

DE 2, north end of bridge which crosses Red Clay Creek at, 4.6 miles from Union Street, Wilmington. (NC 33M)

 WASHINGTON'S FORTIFICATIONS

This ridge was fortified by Washington's Army September 7 and 8, 1777. with cannons "as thick as they could stand."

Upon learning of the fortifications a part of the British Army, then approaching from Iron Hill, took another road, halting at Milltown.

DE 7, east side, five miles from Wilmington. (NC 49M)

 WASHINGTON'S RECONNAISSANCE

Generals Washington, Greene, and Lafayette came to Iron Hill, August 26, 1777, in hope of viewing British Army then landing along the Elk River. Only a few tents could be seen. A heavy storm coming up, they spent the night in a nearby farm house.

Old Baltimore Pike (Rd. 26), north side, one mile west of Cooch's Bridge. (NC 53)

 THE WEDGE

The wedge-shaped tract, west of the Maryland and Delaware curve, consists of approximately 800 acres of land. For more than a century, the property was claimed by Pennsylvania but governed by Delaware. In 1889, a joint commission appointed from both states awarded it to Delaware. This decision was ratified by Pennsylvania in 1897, by Delaware in 1921, and by Congress of the United States in 1921.

o *DE 896, east side, at DE-PA State Line. (NC 36)*
o *DE 273, north side, opposite cemetery of Head of Christiana Church, one and one-half mile west of Newark, near DE-MD State line. (NC 37M)*

WELSH TRACT

Northern boundary line of tract of thirty thousand acres granted to Welsh by William Penn, 1701. It included what is now Pencader Hundred, Delaware, and a part of Cecil County, Maryland.

South College Avenue [Depot Road], west side, 0.7 miles south of Main Street, Newark. (NC 39M)

BUENA VISTA

COOCH'S BRIDGE, NEAR NEWARK

INTERIOR, BUENA VISTA

Buena Vista was built in 1845 by John M. Clayton. He was a noted Delaware statesman and Secretary of State of the United States under two presidents. (See markers 15 and 16, page 25) The **Battle of Cooch's Bridge**, September 3, 1777, is the only Revolutionary War battle fought in Delaware. Tradition holds that the new 13-starred flag, the Stars and Stripes, was first unfurled in the battle. (See marker 7, page 23)

WELSH TRACT

Approximate southern boundary of tract of thirty thousand acres granted by William Penn to the Welsh in 1701. It included what is now Pencader Hundred, Delaware, and a part of Cecil County, Maryland.

DE 896, west side, 10 miles south of Newark, near Mount Pleasant Road. (NC 47)

 WELSH TRACT CHURCH

One-fourth mile southwest is old Welsh Tract Primitive Baptist Meeting House. Congregation organized in Wales, 1701, settled here,1703. A cannon ball passed through Meeting House during Battle of Cooch's Bridge, September 3, 1777.

DE 896, west side, at Welsh Tract Church Road, 2.5 miles south from Newark. (NC 40M)

116 **WILMINGTON**

Founded by Swedes 1638 at Fort Christina, the first permanent settlement in Delaware River Valley. Called Altenae by Dutch 1655. Known as Willingtown 1730-1739. Incorporated as borough of Wilmington in 1739 and as a city in 1832. Washington's Headquarters here in 1777. Became County Seat of New Castle County in 1881.

o *US 13 and New Castle Avenue, south of Third Street Bridge, Wilmington. (NC 62M)*

o *DE 52 [Kennett Pike] and DE 100 [Dupont Road]. (NC 66M)*

o *DE 48 [Lancaster Pike] and Faulkland Road, at Silverbrook Cemetery, south of DE 48 and DE 100 intersection. (NC 67)*

o *Six additional numbered markers (NC 61, 63, 64, 65, 68 and 69) were erected, but no record of their loction is available and these are considered missing.*

 WILMINGTON FRIENDS SCHOOL

The oldest existing school in Delaware, Wilmington Friends was founded in 1748. It resided in the first meeting house of the Wilmington Meeting of the Religious Society of Friends (Quakers) at Fourth and West Streets, which had been built ten years earlier on land given by Elizabeth and William Shipley. The school's original aim was to provide schooling in matters "civil and useful" for Quaker children and "poor children, either black or white."

In its first century, guided by Wilmington Monthly Meeting, the school fulfilled that aim. Delaware's first historian, Benjamin Ferris, wrote in 1846, "Thousands of children have there received the first rudiments of an English education." In its second century, as the state provided public education, Friends became Delaware's first true college preparatory school.

In 1937, having outgrown its much-expanded but aged home, Friends School moved to this site in Alapocas. Though now physically separated from its parent meeting, the school continues to be sustained by the wisdom of that meeting and the teaching of all Quakers that "there is that of God in each of us."

101 School Road, North Wilmington, Alapocas. (NC 107)

LEGISLATIVE HALL ON ST. JONES RIVER, DOVER

Legislative Hall, sitting serenely on the St. Jones River, was built in 1932 and significantly expanded in the 1990's. The Hall includes a display of paintings of former governors and other notable Delawareans.

KENT COUNTY

 BARRATT'S CHAPEL

[Cradle of Methodism in America]

Erected on land deeded by Col. Philip Barratt, August, 1780. Here Thomas Coke, D.D., representative of John Wesley, preached November 14, 1784, administering the Sacrament of Holy Communion for the first time by a Methodist in America. With Francis Asbury planned organization of Methodist Episcopal Church, calling first conference to meet at Baltimore, December 24, 1784.

US 113, east side, 10 miles south of Dover Green. (K 25)

 BELMONT HALL

Built on tract of land called "Pearman's Choice." Home of Thomas Collins, Brigadier General of Kent County Militia during Revolution and Governor of Delaware [1786-1789], who called State Convention in Dover, which on December 7, 1787 was first to ratify the Federal Constitution, thus making Delaware the first state.

US 13, east side, at Rd. 12, just south of Smyrna. (K 32M)

 BETHEL METHODIST CHURCH

The roots of Methodism in this community can be traced to the late 18th century, when Methodist pioneers such as Francis Asbury traveled throughout this area spreading the message of their faith. Over time some church members became dissatisfied with the organization and government of the established Methodist Episcopal Church. As a result, the Methodist Protestant Church was founded in 1830. Soon thereafter a group of local Methodists affiliated with the new church began to meet at or near the homes of its members. In 1838 the congregation was formally organized as Bethel Methodist Protestant Church, being the first of this denomination in Kent County. A church was constructed at this location for the use of the congregation.

It was rebuilt in 1871, extensively remodeled in 1904, and rededicated in 1905.

South side of Rd. 304, west of Rd. 304 and Rd. 114, Andrewville. (K 64)

 BISHOP RICHARD ALLEN

Richard Allen founded and became the first Bishop of the African Methodist Episcopal Church in 1816. Born into slavery in Philadelphia, Pennsylvania, on February 14, 1760, Allen and his family were sold to a family near Dover in 1772. While there, he purchased his freedom, became a minister and joined the Continental Army as a non-combatant during the Revolutionary War. After returning to Philadelphia, he and Sussex countian, Absalom Jones, founded the Free African Society in 1787. He helped organize and was elected president of "The First Convention of the People of Colour" in 1830.

Loockerman Street, near City Hall, Dover. (K 43)

5 BRECKNOCK

In 1680 Alexander Humphreys received a warrant from the county court for 600 acres of land which he called Brecknock. The tract is believed to have been named for a shire in Wales. A milling operation was established here in the 1740's. For nearly two centuries local farmers brought their grain to this place, known for much of that time as Howell's Mill. The present mansion house was constructed in several stages, with the first section believed to have been built by the mid 18th century. Brecknock was listed in the National Register of Historic Places in 1974. In 1993 a portion of the original tract was bequeathed to Kent County by Elizabeth Howell Goggin for recreational use.

Main Street extended, west side, 0.1 mile south of intersection with US 13, Camden. (K 55)

GARDEN, WOODBURN, DOVER

GARDEN, WOODBURN, DOVER

WOODBURN - THE GOVERNOR'S RESIDENCE

Woodburn was built in 1790. This handsome Georgian building has been the official Governor's Residence since 1965.

6   BYFIELD

Near this site stood the boyhood home of Caesar Rodney, signer of the Declaration of Independence. Byfield was originally settled in the early 1680's by Daniel Jones, Rodney's maternal great-grandfather. Following Jones' death, it became the family seat for three generations of the Rodney Family. Caesar Rodney spent his formative years here and eventually acquired ownership of the property after the death of his mother in 1763. Upon entering public life in 1764, Rodney moved to the town of Dover. Although the property was occupied by tenant farmers, Rodney retained Byfield until his death in 1784. He is buried in an unmarked family cemetery on the property.

DE 9, east side, at Bergold Road (Rd. 352), east of Dover Air Force Base, Dover. (K 53)

7   CAESAR RODNEY

Statesman, soldier, and patriot. Member of Stamp Act Congress and of First and Second Continental Congresses. Signer of Declaration of Independence. Member and speaker of Colonial Assembly of "Three Lower Counties on Delaware." Member of Council of Safety, Major General of Delaware Militia, and President [Governor] of Delaware during American Revolution. Born 1728, died 1784. Buried on his farm "Poplar Grove." Reinterred in Christ Churchyard 1887.

US 13, front wall of Episcopal Churchyard [Christ Church], corner of State and Water Streets, Dover. [Bronze Tablet]

8   CAESAR RODNEY

Born on October 7, 1728 on a farm east of Dover, Caesar Rodney was one of Delaware's most distinguished statesman. Entering public life at an early age, Rodney held numerous local offices. He was a member of the Colonial States Assembly, and a delegate to the Stamp Act Congress. From 1774 through 1776 he was a member of the Continental Congress.

During his service as a member of the Continental Congress in 1776, Rodney was summoned from his home to Philadelphia to break a deadlock in the state's delegation and add Delaware to the list of states approving the Declaration of Independence. He was commissioned Brigadier General during the Revolution and given responsibility for commanding the Delaware Militia. In 1778 he was elected President (or Governor) of Delaware, a capacity in which he served until 1781. He died at his home near Dover on June 29, 1784. Throughout his career of public service, Caesar Rodney was noted for his high integrity, purity of character, and patriotic leadership.

In 1916 a new school for area youth was constructed. Named to honor Delaware's patriot hero, the first Caesar Rodney High School was located on Camden-Wyoming Avenue. It was replaced by the present structure in 1967.

Northwest corner of Old Camden Rd./ Main St. and North Rd, Camden. (K 62)

9   CAMDEN

Founded 1783 on the tract "Brecknock" by Daniel Mifflin and settled largely by Quakers. Once called Piccadilly and Mifflins Crossroads. Incorporated 1852, it was a center of antislavery sentiment. Several homes were by tradition stops on the Underground Railroad.

US 13, west side, 300 feet north of junction of DE 10. (K 41)

10   CAPTAIN JONATHAN CALDWELL

This farm, formerly known as Burberry's Berry, was home of Captain Jonathan Caldwell of Colonel Haslet's Regiment in Revolution. Tradition says Delaware soldiers received name "Blue Hen's Chickens" from Caldwell's men having with them game chickens, celebrated in Kent for their famous fighting qualities, the brood of a certain blue hen.

US 13, east side, near junction of Felton and Frederica Roads [DE 12], 10 miles from Dover Green. (K 17)

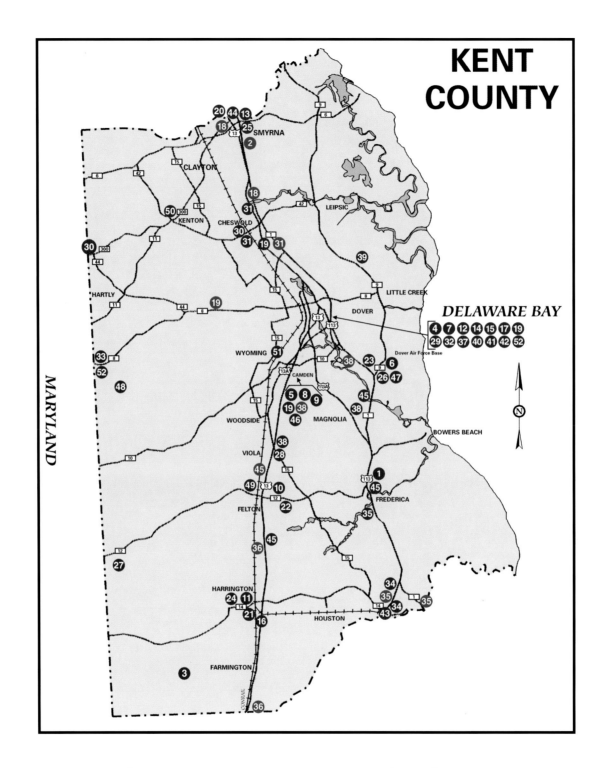

KENT COUNTY

MARYLAND

SMYRNA

CLAYTON

KENTON

CHESWOLD

LEIPSIC

LITTLE CREEK

HARTLY

DOVER

DELAWARE BAY

Dover Air Force Base

WYOMING

CAMDEN

WOODSIDE

MAGNOLIA

BOWERS BEACH

VIOLA

FELTON

FREDERICA

HARRINGTON

HOUSTON

FARMINGTON

Kent County is the central county of Delaware, bordered on the north by New Castle County, the south by Sussex County, the west by Maryland and the east by the Delaware Bay. The state government and a U.S. Air Force Base are major contributors to the local economy.

11 CLARK'S CORNER

On September 17, 1740, Thomas Clark received a Proprietary Warrant from Thomas Penn for lands "adjoining his dwellin place" which he named "Clark's Folly." By the 1790's Benjamin Clark and his son Matthew had established an inn and tavern on this land at a location which became known as Clark's Corner. A mill, store, and blacksmith's shop were located nearby. This was an important stop for travelers. A post office was established here in 1857. On January 31, 1859, the Delaware General Assembly formally changed the name of this community from Clark's Corner to Harrington.

Delaware Avenue, one block north of intersection with Clark Avenue (DE 14), Harrington. (K 47)

12 COLONEL JOHN HASLET

Presbyterian minister, later practiced medicine. Member of Colonial Assembly. Member of Council of Safety, 1775. Commanded First Delaware Militia Regiment. This regiment, reviewed in Dover, later joined Washington's Army, and fought in Battles of Long Island and White Plains. It disbanded December, 1776. Haslet continuing with Washington's Army was killed Battle of Princeton, January 3, 1777. Buried First Presbyterian Churchyard, Philadelphia, reinterred here 1841, when address was delivered by John M. Clayton.

US 13, on front wall of old Presbyterian Church, on Southern Boulevard, opposite Bank Lane, Dover. [Bronze Tablet]

13 COMMODORE JACOB JONES

Born 1768, near this site. Commanded U.S. sloop *Wasp* in notable victory over superior British sloop *Frolic*, October, 1812, off Cape Hatteras. Commanded frigate *Constitution* 1818-1829. Died August, 1850. Buried at Cecilton, Maryland. Reinterred in Wilmington and Brandywine Cemetery, with distinguished honors.

US 13, west side, near East Street, Smyrna. (K 2)

**14 DELAWARE STATE COLLEGE
FIRST COLLEGE FOR BLACKS IN DELAWARE**

Established May 15, 1891, by an act of the Delaware General Assembly as the State College for Colored Students, by virtue of the 1890 Morrill Land-Grant Act and under the provisions of the 1862 Morrill Act of Congress. Incorporated July 1, 1891. Reincorporated March 10, 1911. Name changed to Delaware State College in 1947.

US 13, at entrance to College. (K 42)

15 DELAWARE STATE COLLEGE HIGH SCHOOL

On June 17, 1921, the Board of Trustees of the State College for Colored Students, later known as Delaware State College, approved a resolution recommending the establishment of a four year high school for Negro students on its campus. This was the second such institution in the state, and the first outside of Wilmington. Many of the classes were held in the DuPont Building, also known as the Practice School. The building was named for Pierre S. du Pont, a Delaware philanthropist who was instrumental in funding the construction of Negro schools throughout the state. With the establishment of a comprehensive high school for Negro students in each county, the State College High School was closed in 1952.

Delaware State University, rear of campus, US 13, North Dover. (K 45)

16 DELAWARE STATE FAIR

In 1919 local residents held several meetings to discuss the establishment of a fair. On January 12, 1920, the Kent and Sussex County Fair Association was organized for the purposes of "promoting and encouraging agriculture" and "giving pleasures and deversions to the inhabitants of rural communities." The first fair was held in July, 1920. In 1962 this annual event was named the Delaware State Fair to reflect its popularity and statewide appeal. The grounds

LEGISLATIVE HALL, DOVER

INTERIOR, LEGISLATIVE HALL, DOVER

HOUSE CHAMBERS, DOVER

Legislative Hall is home to Delaware's General Assembly, made up of the Senate and House of Representatives. The General Assembly meets in adjoining chambers on the ground floor. Offices for the Governor, legislators and staff are located on the upper and lower levels of the building.

have also been used for a wide variety of activities and events. German prisoners were housed here during World War II, and regular pari-mutuel harness racing was commenced in 1946.

Front of Fairgrounds, US 13, south of Harrington. (K 51)

17   DOVER

County seat since 1680. William Penn, in 1683, ordered town site laid out and named Dover. Plotted in 1717. Temporary capital in 1777 and permanent capital since 1779. Federal Constitution ratified here in 1787, making Delaware first state in Union. State Constitutional Convention held here in 1791-1792, 1831, 1852, and 1897.

o   *Junction of Forest Street and Division Street with DE 8, near Dover city limits in triangle, one mile west of Dover Green. (K 36)*

o   *East side of South Governor's Avenue, near Lynnhaven Drive at Dover city limits. (K 37)*

o   *East side of South State Street, 0.8 mile south of Dover Green, near US 13. (K 38)*

o   *US 13A (State Street) and Loockerman Street, on Plaza, Dover. (K 35)*

o   *US 13A, west side, north of Silver Lake, near Blue Coat Inn, 1.4 miles north of Dover Green. (K 34)*

18   DUCK CREEK HUNDRED

Originally embraced all lands south of Duck Creek and north of Leipsic Creek from Delaware River to Maryland line. In 1869 western half of hundred was detached and joined to western half of Little Creek Hundred to form Kenton Hundred.

o   *US 13, south of Duck Creek, west side, 12.4 miles north of Dover Green, Smyrna. (K 1M)*

o   *US 13, north of Garrison Lake, east side, 4.4 miles south of Smyrna Crossroads. (K 3M)*

19   EAST DOVER HUNDRED

Originally part of St. Jones Hundred, renamed Dover Hundred 1823, the boundaries being Little Creek on north and St. Jones on south, extending from Delaware River to Maryland line. Dover Hundred was divided 1877 into two hundreds called East Dover Hundred and West Dover Hundred.

o   *US 13 near Rd. 153, west side, 4.4 miles north of Dover Green. (K 9)*

o   *Dover-Marydel Road [DE 8], south side, 3.7 miles from Dover Green. (K 11M)*

o   *US 13, east side, north of 13A, 2.4 miles south of Dover Green. (K 13)*

o   *US 113, east side, north of Moore's Lake, 2.2 miles south of Dover Green. (K 21)*

20   "FIRST IN THE WORLD"
Post # 14 American Legion Ambulance Service

In 1924, the members of the David C. Harrison American Legion Post # 14 initiated the first American Legion ambulance service in the world. Its eighteen founding members were veterans of World War I who volunteered their time to transport the sick and injured to hospitals in Wilmington, Dover, Milford, and beyond. Prior to this time, persons needing medical assistance were transported by train. This practice was often time-consuming and thereby dangerous to patients who were seriously ill and in need of treatment. At the time of its founding, services were provided to a district that extended from Summit Bridge to Milford. Originally located on South Main Street in Smyrna, the service was moved to this location in 1961.

The Post # 14 American Legion Ambulance Service has been in continuous operation since its founding, and now serves an area from the Delaware Bay to the Maryland border, from Collins Beach to Garrison's Lake. Staffed largely by

CUPOLA, OLD STATE HOUSE

OLD STATE HOUSE, DOVER

The **Old State House** is Delaware's symbolic capitol. Completed in 1792, the State House was shared by the State of Delaware and Kent County governments. The building contains period and reproduction furnishings and accessories, an 18th century courtroom and legislative chamber, and an elegant, restored geometrical staircase.

volunteers, the service was responsible for answering more than 25,000 calls for assistance during its first seventy-five years of operation.

South side of Glenwood Avenue (DE 6), two blocks west of US 13 and DE 6, Smyrna. (K 67)

21 FIRST RURAL FREE DELIVERY ROUTE

For many years the National Grange and other organizations interested in the welfare of citizens residing in rural areas advocated the establishment of rural free delivery of mail. In October 1896, the Post Office Department introduced experimental rural delivery in West Virginia. The new service was favorably received, and by June of the following year there were forty-four routes in operation in twenty-nine states.

On October 3, 1898, rural free delivery of mail in Delaware was initiated with the formal establishment of a route originating in Harrington. Joseph G. Peckham was appointed to serve as carrier for the circuit, with an annual salary of $300. The route was seventeen and one quarter miles in length. Approximately 600 families were served.

The establishment of the rural free delivery service resulted in the elimination of many small rural post offices. In 1902 alone, twenty-nine were closed in Delaware. By 1938, some 23,000 offices had been discontinued throughout the United States since the introduction of rural delivery.

Northeast corner of Clark and Commerce Streets, Harrington (K 61)

22 GEOGRAPHIC CENTER OF DELAWARE

In the vicinity of this marker, a Flat Outline Map of the State would be exactly balanced.

In 1989, a curious seventh grader from the Caesar Rodney School District asked where the center of Delaware was located. With the help of his teacher and the Kent County Department of Planning, it was determined that the geographic center of the state was located approximately eleven miles south of Dover in the field just south of this marker, on the Killen Farm.

DE 12, south side, 1.2 miles east of intersection with US 13, Felton. (K 57)

23 HANGAR 1301

Constructed in 1944, Hangar 1301 served as the headquarters and engineering facility for the 4146th Base Unit from 1944 to 1946. Highly secret testing and development work was done here on air-launched rocket weapons. Aircraft used in testing ranged from P-47 Thunderbolts to four-engine bombers including B-17 Flying Fortresses and B-24 Liberators. Even single engine light planes were outfitted with multiple rocket launchers to test the feasibility of providing additional firepower for all types of aircraft.

The main hangar was used to house aircraft that were being fitted with various types of rocket launchers. The attached building was used as the machine shop to build and modify weapon systems, and the small structure nearby was the heating plant. Hangar 1301 is now the home of the Air Mobility Command Museum. The original concrete ramp now serves as the outside display park for the museum. The hangar complex was listed in the National Register of Historic Places in 1994.

Dover Air Force Base, north side US 113, Dover. (K 68)

24 HARRINGTON

Formerly known as Clark's Corner, the roots of this community can be traced to settlement by the Clark family in the 1730's, and the subsequent establishment of an inn, tavern, store, and mill nearby. The village was little more than a country crossroads before the coming of the railroad in 1856. In that same year Matthew J. Clark subdivided a portion of his lands into town lots which would form the nucleus of the growing community. In 1859 the state legislature renamed the town in honor of Judge Samuel M.

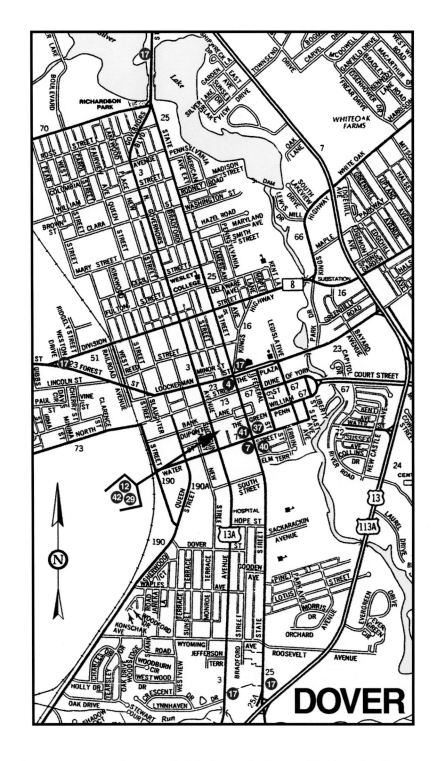

Dover is a charming city and a visual delight, with flower filled parks, historic government buildings, numerous museums, the picturesque Green, and lovely Georgian and Victorian homes.

Harrington, a prime mover in the effort to bring the railroad to southern Delaware. Harrington was incorporated by the General Assembly on March 23, 1869.

o *DE 14, City Limits, east side, Harrington. (K 48)*
o *DE 14, City Limits, west side, Harrington. (K 49)*

 HOME OF ALLEN McLANE

For many years this home was the property of Colonel Allen McLane, statesman and hero of the American Revolution.

Born in Philadelphia August 8, 1746. McLane had moved to Delaware by 1769. His military career began when he was commissioned as an officer in the state militia in 1775. After the outbreak of the Revolution, McLane volunteered to raise a company of troops, investing much of his inheritance in accompanying expenses. During the course of the war he was an active participant in many major engagements including Long Island, White Plains, Trenton, Princeton, and the Siege of Yorktown. His bravery and enterprise were rewarded in 1777 when he received his captain's commission from General Washington. He was one of the first to suspect the loyalty of Benedict Arnold, and is said to have played a significant role in convincing the French to blockade the Chesapeake in 1781. He was a member of the Order of Cincinnati. For many years he was active in the affairs of church and state, serving as Speaker of the State House of Representatives, member of the Privy Council, Judge of the Court of Common Pleas, and U.S. Marshall for Delaware. He was delegate at Delaware's historic Constitution Ratification Convention in 1787, and a long-time advocate of the Methodist church.

Following his return from the war it is believed that the McLane family rented a home at the southwest corner of Mt. Vernon and Market Streets. On December 23, 1785, Allen McLane, "Merchant," received a deed from Thomas Wilds for a parcel of land including the lot where his house stands. Among the members of the family moving to the home was

McLane's infant son Louis, later a distinguished member of Congress, Minister to England, and United States Secretary of State. McLane maintained homes here and on his farm until he moved to Wilmington following his appointment as Port Collector in 1797. He retained ownership of this property until selling it in 1828, one year prior to his death.

40 West Mount Vernon Street, Smyrna. (K 59)

 HOME OF JOHN DICKINSON

"The Penman of the Revolution." Member of Delaware Colonial and State Assemblies. Member of Continental Congress, Annapolis Convention, and Philadelphia Federal Constitutional Convention. Signer for Delaware of Articles of Confederation and Federal Constitution. Governor of Delaware and President, Second Delaware Constitutional Convention. Born Maryland 1732, died Wilmington 1808.

Kitts Hummock Road [Rd. 68], off US 113, south side, at entrance to John Dickinson Mansion. (K 33)

HOME OF JUDGE THOMAS WHITE
Refuge of Francis Asbury

Near this site stood the home of Judge Thomas White, member of the Colonial Maryland Legislature and Delaware House of Assembly, Chief Justice of the Kent County Court of Common Pleas, and delegate to the Delaware Constitutional Conventions of 1776 and 1791-92. This was also the boyhood home of his son, Samuel White, U. S. Senator from Delaware 1801-09. Here the future Methodist Bishop, Francis Asbury, found refuge during the tumultuous Revolutionary War years of 1778-80. While living with the Whites, Asbury developed the ideas that would shape the future of American Methodism.

Whiteleysburg Road (Rd. 59), on right, one mile east from intersection with DE 12, Whiteleysburg. (K 46)

CHRIST EPISCOPAL CHURCH, DOVER

DOVER GREEN, DOVER

CAESAR RODNEY MEMORIAL, DOVER

DOVER

Christ Episcopal Church was built in 1734. A monument to Delaware's **Caesar Rodney**, signer of the Declaration of Independence, is located in the graveyard. Picturesque buildings in **Dover** surround and complement the historic Delaware government buildings.

IMMIGRANT JEWISH FARMS

Delaware's first Jewish farmers, Isaac and Ida Beinoff, settled here in 1897. Like those to follow, they were recent immigrants fleeing poverty and oppression in their native Russia. Between 1912 and 1929, the Jewish Agriculture Society, based in New York City, provided loans to the Beinoffs and other Jewish farmers who moved to Kent County as part of a national "back-to-the-soil" movement. After World War II, the Jewish farmers remaining in the area contributed to the organization of the Jewish community in southern Delaware and the establishment of the first synagogue in Dover.

DE 15, east side of Viola. (K 58)

 JOHN M. CLAYTON

Born in Dagsboro, Delaware, 1796. Graduate of Yale College 1815, member of Delaware House of Representatives 1824, Secretary of State of Delaware 1826-1828. United States Senator 1829-1836, 1845-1849, and 1853 until his death, 1856. Chief Justice of Delaware 1837-1839. United States Secretary of State under Presidents Taylor and Fillmore, 1849 to July, 1850. Negotiated the Clayton-Bulwer Treaty with Great Britain.

US 13, on front wall of old Presbyterian Church, Southern Boulevard, opposite Bank Lane, Dover. [Bronze Tablet]

 KENTON HUNDRED

Created in 1869 by joining of western halves of Duck Creek and Little Creek Hundreds. Is bounded on north by Blackbird Hundred in New Castle County, and on the east by Duck Creek and Little Creek Hundreds, on south by East Dover and West Dover Hundreds, and on west by Maryland line.

o *Cheswold-Kenton Road [DE 42], north side, 6.6 miles from Dover Green. (K 6)*

o *Kenton-Sudlersville Road [DE 300], south side, at Maryland-Delaware line, 16.9 miles from Dover Green. (K 7)*

 LITTLE CREEK HUNDRED

Originally embraced all lands south of Leipsic Creek and north of Little Creek from Delaware River to Maryland line. In 1869 western half of hundred was detached and joined to western half of Duck Creek Hundred to form Kenton Hundred.

o *US 13, west side, south of Garrison's Lake, 7.4 miles from Dover Green. (K 4)*

o *Cheswold-Kenton Road [DE 42], south side, 6.6 miles from Dover Green. (K 5)*

o *US 13, east side, 4.4 miles north of Dover Green. (K 8M)*

 LOOCKERMAN HALL

In 1723 Nicholas Loockerman purchased 600 acres of land known as "The Range." Following his death in 1771, the property passed to his grandson Vincent Loockerman Jr. Evidence suggests that he built the Georgian-style mansion known today as Loockerman Hall soon after inheriting the property. A member of the early Revolutionary-era Committee of Inspection, and county militia, Vincent Loockerman Jr. died on April 5, 1790.

On August 24, 1891, 95 acres of the old plantation where slaves had once toiled were purchased for the purpose of establishing the "Delaware College for Colored Students." Loockerman Hall became the center of the campus, serving variously as a dormitory, classroom, and administration building. In 1971 the structure was placed on the National Register of Historic Places by the National Park Service.

Center of the campus of Delaware State University, West side of US 13, Dover. (K 60)

INTERIOR, RIDGELY HOUSE, DOVER

BIGGS MUSEUM, DOVER

AMERICAN LEGION AMBULANCE SERVICE, SMYRNA

OLD PRESBYTERIAN CHURCH, DOVER

The **Ridgely House** on the Green in Dover was built in 1728. (See marker 41, page 79) The **Sewell C. Biggs Museum,** adjacent to the Green, houses an impressive collection of American Art from the Delaware Valley region. The **Smyrna American Legion Post #14** was the first American Legion to initiate an ambulance service. The **Old Presbyterian Church** was built in 1790 on "Meeting House Square" to replace an earlier log meeting house. In 1950 the church opened as a museum. Colonel John Haslet is buried in the church's graveyard. (See marker 12, page 67)

33 MASON-DIXON CROWN STONE

In 1763, Penn and Calvert commissioners erected milestones along the boundary between Maryland and the Three Lower Counties [Delaware], part of the Mason-Dixon survey. Every five miles they erected elaborate Crown Stones. This stone was displayed in St. Louis in 1904, and later in Baltimore. It was returned to Marydel in 1954 and was reset in 1964.

DE 8, Marydel. (K 69)

34 MILFORD

Town laid out by Joseph Oliver 1787. Village was located on tract then called "Saw-Mill Range." Named Milford from fording place near mill-dam erected by Rev. Sydenham Thorne across Mispillion Creek, 1787. First incorporated 1807. Old town in Kent County, new town in Sussex County. Home of Governors Tharp, Causey, Burton and Watson.

- o *Walnut Street and DE 14, near cemetery, 1.4 miles north from Front Street, Milford. (K 28)*
- o *DE 14 at US 13, north side, one mile from intersection of Front and Walnut Streets, Milford. (K 29)*

35 MILFORD HUNDRED

Originally part of Mispillion Hundred, the boundaries of which were Murderkill Creek on north and Mispillion Creek on south, extending from Delaware River to Maryland line. In 1830 Mispillion Hundred was divided into two hundreds, the western retaining the name Mispillion and the eastern being named Milford Hundred.

- o *US 113, west side, south of Murderkill River, 12.2 miles south of Dover Green. (K 27)*
- o *US 113, east side, north of Haven Lake, 19.3 miles south of Dover Green. (K 30M)*
- o *Milford-Lewes Road [DE 1], east side, 19 miles south of Dover Green. (K 31M)*

36 MISPILLION HUNDRED

Originally embraced all lands south of Murderkill Creek and north of Mispillion Creek from Delaware River to Maryland line. In 1830 was divided into two approximately equal parts, the eastern part being called Milford Hundred and the western part retaining the name Mispillion.

- o *US 13, west side, 13.5 miles south of Dover Green. (K 19M)*
- o *US 13, east side, 23.5 miles south of Dover Green, at Kent and Sussex County line. (K 20M)*

37 NICHOLAS RIDGELY

In this church yard lie the remains of Nicholas Ridgely, statesman and jurist. Born in Dover, 1762, eldest son of Doctor Charles Greenbury Ridgely and Mary Wynkoop Ridgely. Member of State Convention which ratified the Federal Constitution, December 7, 1787. Repeatedly member of General Assembly from 1788 until 1801. Attorney General of Delaware, 1791-1801. Delegate to Second State Constitutional Convention, 1791-92. Chancellor of Delaware from 1801 until his death, 1830.

US 13, front wall of Episcopal Churchyard [Christ Church], corner of State and Water Streets, Dover. [Bronze Tablet]

38 NORTH MURDERKILL HUNDRED

Formerly part of Murderkill Hundred, originally called Motherkill Hundred, kill meaning creek in Dutch. Original boundaries were St. Jones Creek on north, and Murderkill Creek on south, extending from Delaware River to Maryland line. In 1867 Murderkill Hundred was divided into two hundreds named North Murderkill Hundred and South Murderkill Hundred.

- o *US 13, west side, 2.5 miles south of Dover Green. (K 14M)*
- o *US 13, east side, near Canterbury Road, 8.4 miles south of Dover Green. (K 15)*

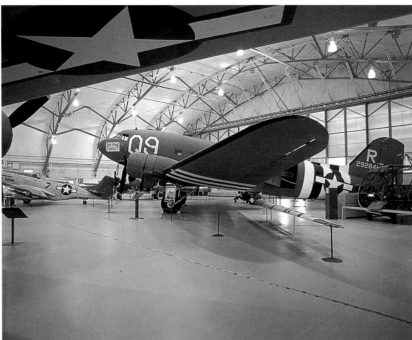

The **Air Mobility Command Museum**, located on Dover Air Force Base features a growing collection of rare vintage aircraft and artifacts. (See marker 23, page 71)

o   *US 113, west side, south of Moore's Lake, 2.3 miles south of Dover Green. (K 22M)*

o   *US 113A, east side, near Rd. 106, 6.3 miles south of Dover Green. (K 23)*

39   OCTAGONAL SCHOOL HOUSE

Among the earliest of the schools opened in Kent County under the Free School Law of 1829. Built about 1836 of undressed stone, designed by Manlove Hayes, an early educator, the school was in use until 1930. Girls and boys sat at benches in rows facing in opposite directions. The outside row faced the wall.

DE 9 between Rd. 86 and Rd. 338, in front of school. (K 40)

40   OLD CHRIST CHURCH

Founded as a mission by the Society for the Propagation of the Gospel in the Gospel in response to a petition from twenty-two inhabitants of Dover in 1703. The present church was erected in 1734. Among early missionaries here was the Rev. Charles Inglis, later first Bishop of Nova Scotia.

South State Street, east side, at Water Street, one block south of Dover Green, Dover. (K 39)

41   RIDGELY HOUSE
Built 1728

Doctor Charles Greenbury Ridgely: member Colonial and State Legislative Assemblies; delegate first State Constitutional Convention 1776. Nicholas Ridgely [the younger]: member of convention that ratified Federal Constitution 1787; delegate second State Constitutional Convention 1791-92; Attorney General 1791-1801; Chancellor of Delaware 1801-1830. Henry Moore Ridgely: three times Secretary of State of Delaware; Representative in Congress 1811-1815; United States Senator 1827-1829. Edward Ridgely: jurist; Secretary of State of Delaware 1859-1863.

House stands on north side of Dover Green. [Bronze Tablet]

42   SITE OF KING GEORGE'S TAVERN

From 1724 known as King George's Tavern. On its sign was painted King George's portrait, supplanted, during the Revolution, by portrait of George Washington. For many years the old hostelry was the meeting place for political rallies and used for gubernatorial receptions.

South side of Dover Green on front wall of Kent County Court House. [Bronze Tablet]

43   SITE OF MILFORD'S FIRST METHODIST CHURCH

The beginning of Methodism in this community can be traced to the organization of a local "society" in 1777. Early meetings were held in the homes of its members. On December 3, 1787, Joseph Oliver conveyed a lot of ground at this location for the purpose of "building a preaching house or church" for the Methodists. A frame chapel was constructed here and completed in 1790. The growth and prosperity of the congregation resulted in the construction of an addition to the church in 1800. Prominent visitors included Methodist pioneers Francis Asbury and Freeborn Garrettson.

The building continued to serve the congregation until 1842, when a new church was constructed across the street at the northwest corner of Third and North Streets. The old building was then sold and moved. Interments here had commenced in the late 18th century, and following removal of the first church, the site was used exclusively as a burial ground for members. Notable burials include those of Peter F. Causey, Governor of Delaware (1855-1859), and Civil War General Alfred T. A. Torbert.

East side of North Street at Third Street, Milford. (K 65)

44   SITE OF OLD ASBURY METHODIST CHURCH

The roots of Methodism in this community can be traced to the organization of a local "society" in the 1770's. Meetings were held in private homes before a frame structure was

JOHN DICKINSON PLANTATION

JOHN DICKINSON PLANTATION

JOHN DICKINSON PLANTATION, INTERIOR

JOHN DICKINSON PLANTATION

John Dickinson Plantation, south of Dover, is a Delaware State Museum site for the interpretation of 18th-century Kent County plantation life. Visitors will see guides in period clothing demonstrating cooking, weaving and many other aspects of Delaware in the 18th century . John Dickinson (1732-1808) was known as the "Penman of the Revolution" for his writings in support of independence from England. (See marker 26, page 73)

built here circa 1786 on land provided by Col. Allan McLane, Revolutionary War hero and early advocate of Methodism. On May 9, 1799, the meeting house and burial ground were formally conveyed to the church trustees for 5 shillings. The Philadelphia Annual Conference was held here on numerous occasions in the late 18th and early 19th centuries. Francis Asbury and many other Methodist pioneers were frequent visitors. Services were held here until 1845, when the congregation relocated to a new site, and the old church was dismantled and moved.

Delaware Street, west side, between Mt. Vernon and North Streets, Smyrna. (K 56)

45 SOUTH MURDERKILL HUNDRED

Formerly part of Murderkill Hundred, originally called Motherkill Hundred, kill meaning creek in Dutch. Original boundaries were St. Jones Creek on north and Murderkill Creek on south, extending from Delaware River to Maryland line. In 1867 Murderkill Hundred was divided into two hundreds named North Murderkill Hundred and South Murderkill Hundred.

o *US 13, west side, 9.3 miles south of Dover Green. (K 16M)*

o *US 13, east side, 13.4 miles south of Dover Green. (K 18)*

o *US 113, west side, near Rd.106, 6.3 miles south of Dover Green. (K 24)*

o *US 113, east side, north of Murderkill Creek, 12.1 miles south of Dover Green. (K 26)*

46 STAR HILL A.M.E. CHURCH

By the end of the 18th century this area was home to a large number of African Americans, many of them freed slaves. Their settlement was largely due to the efforts of local Quakers. A congregation of the African Methodist Episcopal Church was established here circa 1863. On June 12, 1866, the congregation purchased land from Henry W. Postles as the site for their church, which they named "Star of the East."

Members of the church are believed to have participated in the activities of the Underground Railroad, and the church's name is attributed to the symbol of the star as a guide for escaping slaves.

Rd 360, south of Camden, 1/4 mile east of US 13. (K 50)

47 ST. JONES NECK
Site of Settlement in the 1660's

This part of what is now Kent County, Delaware was one of the state's earliest sites of English colonization. Beginning in the 1660's, plantations were established along the St. Jones River. The Dickinson family of Talbot County, Maryland was among the families who obtained early land patents in this area. Parts of "Merritts," "Whartons" and "Youngs" tracts were among the lands purchased by the Dickinsons with pounds of tobacco.

Kitts Hummock Road [Rd. 68], in front of Dickinson Plantation, off US 113. (K 44)

48 THOMAS' CHAPEL
[Chapeltown]

The site of one of the earliest Methodist churches in America, the first structure was built in 1761 as an Episcopal Church. Built of logs, the church was referred to as the Log or Forest Chapel. According to tradition, ownership of the structure passed to the Methodists in the late 1770's. The church was renamed Thomas' Chapel to honor William Thomas, a local Methodist leader who was instrumental in securing the church building. A frame structure replaced the log church in the late 18th century and the first brick building was erected in 1825. Major renovations took place in the late 1870's. Thomas' Chapel was placed on the National Register of Historic Places on January 26, 1994.

Westville Road (Rd. 206) and Sandy Bend Road (Rd. 222), three miles east of Marydel, Chapeltown. (K 52)

BYFIELD, OUTSIDE OF DOVER

THE ALLEE HOUSE

LOOCKERMAN HALL

BARRATT'S CHAPEL

Byfield is the location of the boyhood home of Caesar Rodney. He is believed to be buried on the property in an unmarked grave. (See Marker 6, page 65) **Loockerman Hall**, a Georgian-style mansion, is now the center of the campus of Delaware State University in Dover. (See marker 32, page 75) The **Allee House** is a well-preserved plantation house that was built around 1753 and is part of the Bombay Hook Wildlife Refuge. **Barratt's Chapel** was erected in 1780, and is known as the "Cradle of Methodism in America." (See marker 1, page 63)

TOWN OF FELTON

The town of Felton was laid out in 1856 when the Delaware Railroad reached this area. Located between Berrytown to the west and Johnny Cake Landing [Frederica] to the east, the town became a "whistle" stop on the new railroad line. Owing its existence to the railroad, Felton was named in honor of Samuel M. Felton, President of the Philadelphia, Wilmington and Baltimore Railroad and a major force in bringing railroad service to central and southern Delaware. Incorporated on February 2, 1861, Felton's boundaries formed a one-half mile square with the railroad line running north-south through the middle of town. Passenger rail service to Felton ended in the early 1950's.

Main Street (DE 12), north side, at Railroad Crossing, Felton.
(K 54)

 TOWN OF KENTON

The origin of this community can be traced to the mid-18th century, when growing travel between Dover and the head of the Chester River resulted in the establishment of a Public House here to support the needs of travelers. Increasing commerce led to the growth of settlement. First known as Grog-Town and Lewis' Cross Roads, the village was formally named Kenton in 1806.

A post office was established here in 1857. With the arrival of the Maryland and Delaware Railroad following the Civil War, the town became an important shipping point for local goods and products. By the 1880s the town was home to 300 residents and a number of thriving businesses. On April 22, 1887, the Town of Kenton was formally incorporated by the Delaware General Assembly.

North side of Rd. 300, at Town Hall, Kenton. (K 66)

51   TOWN OF WYOMING

The construction of the Delaware Railroad in the 1850's led to the establishment of the Delmarva Peninsula's first and most important north-south railway transportation artery. Proximity to the nearby community of Camden resulted in the location of a station here when the railroad arrived in 1856. Settlement of "West Camden" quickly expanded with the construction of homes and businesses. In 1865 the Rev. John J. Pierce migrated here from the Wyoming Valley in Pennsylvania. Rev. Pierce purchased lands and subdivided them into building lots. Other residents of Wyoming Valley followed Rev. Pierce and settled in and around the thriving village. Desiring to sever any shared identity or connection with Camden, residents chose to honor the new citizens by changing the name of the community to Wyoming. A post office was established in 1866, and in 1869 the town of Wyoming was incorporated by the Delaware General Assembly. Surrounded by some of the state's most-productive farmlands, the town of Wyoming was a major point for the shipping of peaches and other agricultural products.

Wyoming, Railroad Ave., 1/2 block north of Camden-Wyoming and Railroad Avenues. (K 63)

 WEST DOVER HUNDRED

Originally part of St. Jones Hundred, renamed Dover Hundred, 1823, the boundaries being Little Creek on north and St. Jones Creek on south, extending from Delaware River to Maryland line. Dover Hundred was divided 1877 into two hundreds, called West Dover Hundred and East Dover Hundred.

o   *Dover-Marydel Road [DE 8] and Rd. 104, north side at Dover Country Club, 2.2 miles from Dover Green. (K 8)*
o   *Dover-Marydel Road [DE 8], south side in Marydel just east of DE-MD State Line, 13.9 miles from Dover Green. (K 12)*

Georgetown is the county seat of Sussex County by virtue of its central location. The center of town is the "Circle," dominated by the red brick Greek Revival courthouse built in 1839.

SUSSEX COUNTY

 ABBOTT'S MILL

The origin of Abbott's Mill can be traced to the fall of 1795 when local carpenter Nathan Willey entered into a contract to purchase land at this location. On April 23, 1802, Willey and several of his neighbors presented a petition to the Court of General Sessions stating that he had "at a large expense erected, and just finished" a grist mill on the site. Citing the many advantages to the citizens of the neighborhood, the petition requested that a new road be extended to the recently-completed mill.

Following Willey's death in 1812 the mill was sold to James Owens, and then to Issac Riggs. From 1821 until 1874 it was owned by members of the Johnson family, and while the property passed through the hands of several subsequent owners, it was known as "Johnson's Mill" until it was purchased by miller Ainsworth Abbott in 1919. The core of the present mill building is believed to have been constructed on the foundation of the original structure during the latter portion of the 19th century.

The mill was operated by Mr. Abbott until shortly before the State of Delaware began the acquisition of the property in 1963. Abbott's Mill was listed in the National Register of Historic Places in 1972. Adjoining property was added to the Register in 1979. The site is now a part of the Delaware Nature Society's Abbott's Mill Nature Center, which offers programs and activities designed to foster a greater understanding and appreciation of our natural environment.
North side of Rd. 620, 0.2 miles east of Rd. 620 and Rd. 633, 2 miles southwest of Milford. (S 125)

 ABSALOM JONES
1746-1818

Born near this place on a plantation known as "Cedar Town," Jones moved to Philadelphia in 1762 and in 1784 purchased

his freedom. He helped to establish the Free African Society in 1787. A leader of the independent African-American church movement, in 1792 he organized St. Thomas' African Episcopal Church [Philadelphia] and in 1804 became the first African-American to be ordained an Episcopal priest. He fervently opposed slavery and other forms of social injustice.
DE 36 and DE 1, Milford. (S 81)

 ACADEMY / MASONIC HALL

In 1827 the Delaware legislature authorized a lottery for the purpose of funding the construction of "an Academy and Masonic Hall." Land was purchased in 1840, and construction commenced the following year. The building was formally dedicated on December 28, 1842. The Georgetown Academy had a prestigious reputation and was attended by students from throughout the county. Classes at this private institution were discontinued in 1885 when a new public school was built in the town. In 1889 the Trustees of the Academy conveyed their interest in the property to Franklin Lodge # 12. The building was remodeled to its present appearance in 1920.
East Market Street and North Railroad Avenue, northeast corner, Georgetown. (S 95)

 ANTIOCH CAMP MEETING

In 1890 the Trustees of Antioch African Methodist Episcopal Church purchased land for the construction of a new house of worship. Annual camp meetings were soon established. Known as "Big Camp" or "Frankford Camp," people traveled from miles around to attend. Covered wagons were used for shelter prior to the construction of wooden "tents." Cooking was done in large iron containers called 'hogkilling pots." Light was provided by "firestands" prior to the use of electricity. Visitors ate at the "Boarding House" and

Return Day is celebrated in Georgetown every two years. This occurs two days after Election Day, when winning and losing candidates get together to "bury the hatchet" and enjoy the festivities. (See marker 80, page 119)

"Confectionary." Worship services were held in the "Bower," a covered meeting place in the center of the grounds. Many of the original buildings were destroyed by fire in 1943.

Clayton Street, west side, 0.2 mile north of Hickory Street, Frankford. (S 93)

5 ASBURY UNITED METHODIST CHURCH

On May 16, 1812, land at this location was conveyed by Minos and Sally Tindall to representatives of the local Methodist society "in trust that they shall build or cause to be erected thereon a house or place of worship for the use of the members of the Methodist Episcopal Church." The church was formally incorporated as Asbury Chapel following an election of trustees held here on March 20, 1813. It is one of many in the state which are named in honor of noted Methodist pioneer Francis Asbury.

Following damage by fire, the aforementioned structure was replaced by the present building in 1857. There have been several major renovations of the sanctuary since that time. The Church School addition was completed in 1957. Construction of the Community Building was commenced after additional property was given to the church by William E. and Julia J. Tyndall in 1947. The Community Building was expanded following the purchase of adjoining land in 1958. A short distance away was the location of Tindall's Camp Meeting Ground.

North side of Rd. 9 at Rd. 446, 5.5 miles southwest of Georgetown. (S 123)

6 BALTIMORE HUNDRED

Prior to 1775 this hundred was claimed as part of Worcester County, Maryland, being named for Lord Baltimore. After the boundary line between Maryland and Delaware was confirmed, Baltimore Hundred became part of Sussex County, Delaware.

o *US 113, west side, 17.8 miles from Georgetown Circle. (S 23M)*

o *US 113, east side, at DE-MD State Line, 21.4 miles from Georgetown Square. (S 24M)*

o *DE 26, south side, 2.6 miles from center of Dagsboro. (S 62M)*

7 BETHANY UNITED METHODIST CHURCH
(Lowe's Crossroads)

In the early part of the twentieth century, members of the Old Jones' Methodist Church began to search for a more central location for the congregation to worship. Although the land for the new church was donated by Sarah C. Collins in 1914, construction of the building had already begun the previous year. Incorporated on March 5, 1914, the church was named Bethany Methodist Episcopal Church. The name was reportedly taken from the church attended by department store pioneer John Wanamaker, who had made a donation toward the completion of this church. Dedicated in June of 1914, the church added the Community Hall during the 1920's.

Lowe's Crossroads, 0.5 mile south of DE 24 and Rd. 421 intersection. (S 105)

8 BETHEL CHURCH

During the late 18th century, Methodist itinerants traveled throughout the peninsula. Their efforts were well-received in rural areas such as this, described as "the heart of Methodism" in the 1780's. The seeds sown by those early travelers continued to bear fruit as membership increased and congregations multiplied. On February 23, 1841, a group of local Methodists purchased land where "a meeting house," called Bethel, had been erected. By the end of the 19th century, annual camp meetings were being held. Bethel Church continues to be a center of worship, serving this rural community in the spirit of the founders of Methodism.

Rd. 419 and Rd. 415, south of Gumboro, on Delaware-Maryland State Line. (S 97)

Return Day is traditionally highlighted by reading the election results for Sussex County. The festivities include a parade that pairs winners and losers of all state and county elections in horse-drawn carriages and antique autos, followed by speeches and revelry. (See marker 80, page 119)

9 BETHEL CHURCH

Francis Asbury established a congregation at home of White Brown in this vicinity in 1778. The original church known as Brown's Chapel, was built 1781, completed 1806 by White Brown, Lemuel Davis, and Jacob Kinder. Early preachers here were Bishop Asbury, Freeborn Garrettson, and Dr. Coke. Present church built 1895.

DE 18 to DE-MD State Line, continue to Harper Road, MD., and go 1.5 miles to Church on Harper Road. (S 64M)

10 BETHEL SHIPYARD

With the incorporation of the Lewisville Marine Railway Company in 1871, Bethel's reputation as a center for ship repair and construction was firmly established. Approximately 40 vessels were built here before the last ship was launched in 1918. Many were "sailing rams," uniquely designed and among the largest type of sailing vessels constructed in the Chesapeake Bay area.

Rd. 492A, next to Broad Creek Bridge, Bethel. (S 79)

11 BETHESDA METHODIST CHURCH

During the late 18th century many of the residents of this area embraced the Methodist faith. Meetings were often held in the homes of church members. The origin of the Bethesda congregation can be traced to February of 1832, when trustees purchased one half acre of land southeast of here. The land was conveyed by local mill owner Joshua Morris "in trust and confidence" that they erect "a house or place of worship for the use of the members of the Methodist Episcopal Church." In 1895, the existing church building was moved to this site and rebuilt. On January 25, 1896, the trustees received the deed for the land "where Bethesda Church now stands."

East of US 113 on Rd. 326, 0.2 miles north of Rd. 326 and Rd. 432, near Stockley. (S 112)

12 BLADES UNITED METHODIST CHURCH

Formerly known as Cannon's Chapel, the first church building was constructed in the early 1870's on East High Street [then known as Concord Road]. The church was incorporated on July 16, 1877. In 1887, the Trustees of the Church purchased land at the present site on Main Street from the heirs of James M. Blades. A new structure was built and dedicated on January 13, 1889. In honor of Rev. William Benson Gregg, the church was renamed the Gregg Methodist Episcopal Church. Incorporated again on January 26, 1921, the church was remodeled, expanded, and renamed Blades Methodist Episcopal Church. In 1972, the name Blades United Methodist Church was adopted.

Market Street, east side, near 4th Street, Blades. (S 100)

13 THE BRICK HOTEL

This locally famous landmark was constructed in 1836 by Joshua S. Layton and Caleb B. Sipple, builders of the Sussex County Courthouse across the Square. It replaced a frame Public House that had stood on the site. County courts were held here during construction of the courthouse 1837-39. The accommodations and hospitality of the house made this a popular stopping place for both residents and visitors to the county seat.

Known for a time as the Union Hotel, this was a well-known gathering-place for Northern sympathizers during the Civil War. After the war, business flourished with the coming of the railroad. With the advent of the automobile, the number of lodgers began to decline, and the hotel was closed in the mid-1950s. The building was later renovated and used as a bank until 1998. The Brick Hotel was listed in the National Register of Historic Places in 1979.

Southwest corner of West Market St. and The Circle, Georgetown. (S 139)

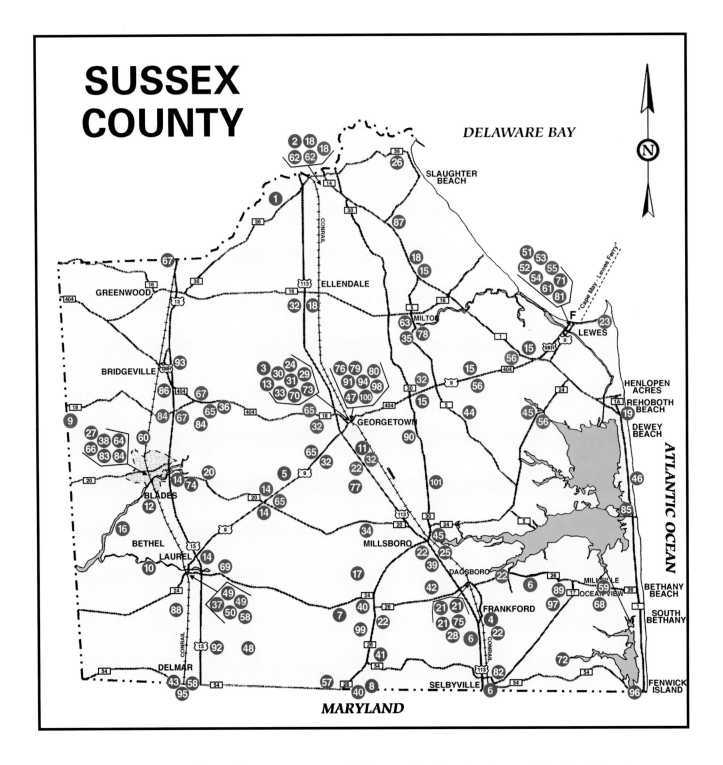

SUSSEX COUNTY

DELAWARE BAY

SLAUGHTER BEACH

GREENWOOD

ELLENDALE

MILTON

LEWES

BRIDGEVILLE

GEORGETOWN

HENLOPEN ACRES

REHOBOTH BEACH

DEWEY BEACH

BLADES

BETHEL

LAUREL

MILLSBORO

DAGSBORO

FRANKFORD

MILLVILLE

OCEAN VIEW

BETHANY BEACH

SOUTH BETHANY

DELMAR

SELBYVILLE

FENWICK ISLAND

ATLANTIC OCEAN

MARYLAND

Sussex County is the southernmost county of Delaware, bordered to the north by Kent County, on the west and south by Maryland, and on the east by the Delaware Bay and the Atlantic Ocean. The majority of the county is characterized by farmland and delightful little towns with yesteryear charm. The coastal area features many water-oriented homes and resorts.

BROAD CREEK HUNDRED

Named after branch of Nanticoke River, and originally extended to southern boundary of Delaware. In 1873, General Assembly detached southern part to become part of Gumboro Hundred.

- o *US 9 and DE 20, north side, 7.3 miles from Georgetown Circle. (S 44M)*
- o *US 13, west side, south of Nanticoke River, 15.2 miles from Georgetown Circle via Concord. (S 7M)*
- o *DE 20 and US 9. (S 45M)*
- o *US 13, east side, 14.1 miles from Georgetown Circle. (S 9M)*

 BROADKILN HUNDRED

Originally known as Broadkill Hundred, after creek of that name, kill being Dutch word for creek. Name changed by General Assembly 1833 when Georgetown Hundred was set off. In 1835 Act was repealed, and Broadkiln Hundred embraced same territory as before 1833. Georgetown Hundred again set off in 1861.

- o *DE 1, south of Waples Pond, 21.6 miles from Georgetown Circle via Belltown. (S 28M)*
- o *DE 1, east side, north of Red Mill Pond, 14.3 miles from Georgetown Circle via Belltown. (S 29)*
- o *US 9, south side, 5.2 miles from Georgetown Circle. (S 38)*
- o *US 9, north side, 8.5 miles from Georgetown Circle. (S 39)*

 CANNON'S FERRY

Isaac and Betty Cannon began operating ferry here on Nanticoke River, February 2, 1793. Their sons continued it, built stores and warehouses in the hamlet named for them. The ferry became property of Sussex County following the brothers death in 1843. First post office, named "Woodland," was established in 1882 and the hamlet took the same name. The state acquired the county roads and ferry in 1935.

Rd. 79 and Rd. 78, north of Bethel, Woodland. (S 65)

 CAREY'S CAMP

By the late eighteenth century a Methodist society had been organized in this area. In 1888, two years after the construction of Carey's Church, the first official Carey's Camp Meeting was held in the grove adjoining the church. These first meetings, known as bush or basket meetings, were held under temporary shelters made of boughs lashed together. The camp now consists of a series of cottages or "tents" which circle an open frame structure called The Tabernacle. Annual worship services are held here for two weeks during the summer. Carey's Camp was placed on the National Register of Historic Places in 1973.

Rd. 421, one mile west of DE 24, four miles south of DE 24 and US 113 intersection, Millsboro. (S 98)

 CEDAR CREEK HUNDRED

Originally known as Cedar Hook Hundred. Before 1683 that part of hundred lying north of Cedar Creek formed part of St. Jones County, now Kent County. When Mispillion Creek was made northern boundary of Sussex County, the northern part of present hundred was consolidated with southern part lying between Cedar Creek and Primehook Creek.

- o *DE 1, west side, 31 miles from Georgetown Circle via Belltown. (S 25M)*
- o *DE 1, east side, north of Waples' Pond, 21.8 miles from Georgetown Circle via Belltown. (S 27)*
- o *US 113, east side, 8 miles from Georgetown Circle. (S 15)*
- o *US 113, west side, south of Haven Lake, 16.6 miles north from Georgetown Circle. (S 13)*

FARM BUILDINGS, GOVERNOR ROSS PLANTATION

SLAVE QUARTERS, GOVERNOR ROSS PLANTATION

GOVERNOR ROSS MANSION

The **Governor Ross Mansion** is an 185''s-era plantation that features the mansion, a fine example of Italianate architecture, a granary, carriage house, and unique renovated log slave quarters. The latter is the only registered slave quarters in Delaware. (See marker 38, page 101)

19   CITY OF REHOBOTH BEACH

On January 27, 1873, the "Rehoboth Beach Camp Meeting Association of the Methodist Episcopal Church" was incorporated by the Delaware Legislature for the purpose of establishing "a permanent camp meeting ground and Christian sea-side resort." With the coming of the railroad in 1878, the growth of the community was accelerated. On March 19, 1891, an act was passed incorporating the municipality as Cape Henlopen City. The name was formally changed to Rehoboth in 1893. Since its founding, the City of Rehoboth Beach has continued to be one of the most popular resorts on the Atlantic Coast, attracting thousands of visitors each year.

Rehoboth Avenue and Boardwalk, Rehoboth. (S 90)

20   CONCORD UNITED METHODIST CHURCH

On August 24, 1804, the Trustees of the Concord Methodist Meeting House purchased this site from Robert Boyce and his wife Nancy. Part of a larger tract known as "New Ireland," the land consisted of approximately three-eights of an acre on which a meeting house had already been erected. In the early 1840's a new structure replaced the original church building. During this same period, it is believed that the cemetery was established. The present building was constructed in 1870. The structure has been remodeled and enlarged several times. The church was formally incorporated in November 22, 1872.

DE 20A, west side, 0.2 mile north of DE 20 and DE 20A intersection, Concord. (S 110)

21   DAGSBORO

East of town is site of mansion of John Dagworthy, officer in British Army in French and Indian War, Brigadier General of Sussex County Militia in American Revolution. Owned tract 20,000 acres called "Dagworthy's Conquest." Dagsboro is birthplace of John M. Clayton, Secretary of State under Presidents Taylor and Fillmore.

o *US 113 and DE 26, 14.7 miles from Georgetown Circle. (S 21M)*

o *DE 26 and Rd. 334, center of Dagsboro, 15.5 miles south of Georgetown Circle. (S 59)*

o *DE 26 and Frankford Road, eastern end of town, 15.7 miles from Georgetown Circle. (S 60)*

22   DAGSBORO HUNDRED

Named after General John Dagworthy. Prior to 1775 was claimed by Province of Maryland. In 1873 General Assembly created Gumboro Hundred out of southern parts of Dagsboro Hundred and Broad Creek Hundred.

o *US 113, west side, 4.4 miles from Georgetown Circle. (S 20M)*

o *US 113, east side, 17.8 miles south of Georgetown Circle. (S 22)*

o *DE 24, east side, 7.1 miles southwest of Millsboro. (S 56)*

o *DE 24, west side, south of Indian River, Millsboro (S 52M)*

o *DE 26, north side, 2.5 miles from center of Dagsboro. (S 61M)*

23   DELAWARE BREAKWATER QUARANTINE STATION
1884-1926

Part of the National Quarantine System established in 1880. Immigrants and ship's crew were inspected for symptoms of diseases. Those showing symptoms of contagious diseases were removed to the station hospital and the ship quarantined for up to 60 days. It was dismantled in 1926 and the land returned to the State of Delaware in 1939.

Rd. 19, Cape Henlopen State Park. (S 75M)

24   DELAWARE TECHNICAL AND COMMUNITY COLLEGE

Site of the first community college in the State of Delaware. Formerly William C. Jason High School, this college was

The **Forty and Eight Boxcar** was one of forty-nine given to the American people by the citizens of France in thanks for aid rendered during and after World War II. Utilized for hauling military cargo during two world wars, they were known for their complement of "forty men-eight horses". (See marker 27, page 95)

created by the Delaware General Assembly in 1966 and opened the doors to students in September 1967. Because of its central location, the southern campus is known throughout Sussex County as "The College."

US 113 and DE 18, Georgetown. (S 76)

25 DICKERSON CHAPEL, A. M. E. CHURCH

On May 2, 1868, the African Methodist Episcopal Church purchased land west of Millsboro from John M. Burton and the first church building was soon built. In 1885, the church officially changed its name to Dickerson Chapel to honor Bishop William Fisher Dickerson. Known locally as the Old Field Church, the church building was renovated and rebuilt several times during the early part of the 20th century. In 1923, Juba Boyce willed land at this site to the church. The congregation moved to this location in 1970 when the present Dickerson Chapel was built under the leadership of Rev. E. L. Coleman.

US 113, east side, 1.25 miles south of DE 24, Millsboro. (S 102)

26 FORT SAULSBURY

Constructed in 1917 as a coastal defense fortification of the U. S. Army. Named for Willard Saulsbury, U. S. Senator from Delaware 1859-1871. Two batteries were located within the fort, each with two 12-inch gun emplacements. The north battery was named for Col. David Hall and the south for Col. John Haslet, heroes of the Revolution. Following removal of the guns during World War II, the fort was converted into a Prisoner of War Camp. Up to 300 prisoners were housed here at a time, providing labor for a variety of local agricultural activities. Fort Saulsbury was deactivated in 1946 and sold as surplus property in 1948.

DE 36, south side, three miles east of DE 1 and DE 36 intersection, near Slaughter Beach.   (S 89)

27 FORTY & EIGHT BOXCAR

This car is one of 49 given to the American people by the citizens of France in thanks for aid rendered during and after World War II. Utilized for hauling military cargo during two world wars, they were known for their complement of "forty men-eight horses." The "Merci" or Gratitude Train was assembled by French veterans, who decorated each car with the coats of arms of the provinces of France. On February 12, 1949, the citizens of Delaware formally welcomed the gift-laden offering at a ceremony held in Wilmington. A statewide exhibition tour followed. The car is owned and maintained by the American Legion's Society of the 40 & 8, Voiture #1320.

Front Street, west side, near corner of Front and Popular Streets, Seaford. (S 94)

28 FRANKFORD UNITED METHODIST CHURCH

In 1819, a group of Methodists purchased a parcel of land north of present-day Frankford. A frame chapel was erected, and on March 4, 1820, the members of the congregation met there to elect trustees and formally organize themselves as Antioch Methodist Episcopal Church. The members purchased the present site on November 20, 1852. The sanctuary was formally dedicated on August 28, 1853. The church was later renamed Frankford Methodist Episcopal Church.

In 1880, a new spire was added, and in 1889, the roof was elevated six feet. Leaded stained glass windows were added during this period. They are considered to be fine examples of the American Opalescent style of the late 19th century. An addition was constructed in 1916 and subsequently expanded with the completion of a second story in 1947. A fellowship hall was built in 1967.

Main Street and Clayton Avenue, Frankford. (S 137)

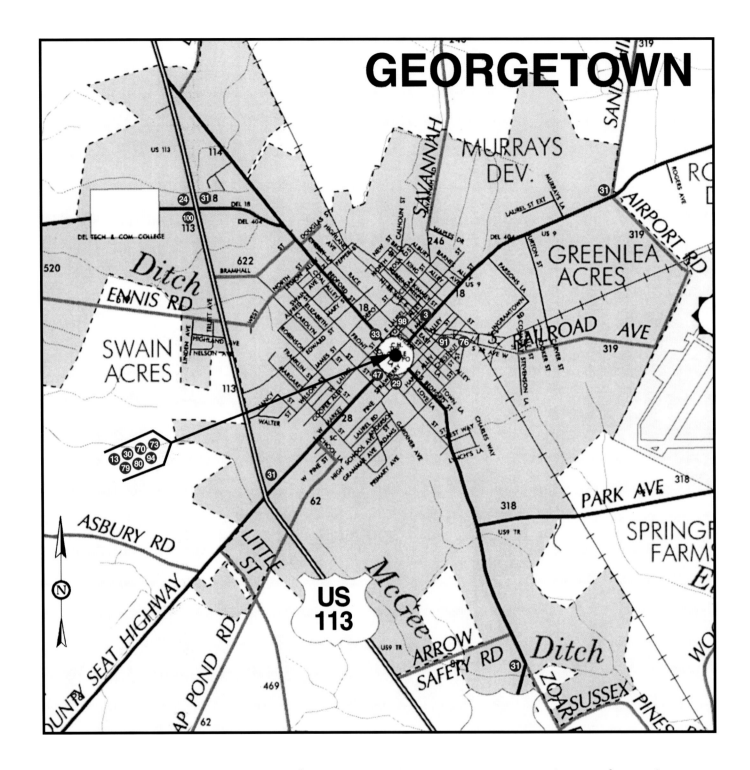

GEORGETOWN

Georgetown was laid out to be the county seat of Sussex County, in accordance with Act of General Assembly of January 29, 1791. It is believed to have been named Georgetown in honor of George Mitchell, who was, for several sessions, Speaker of the State Senate. (See marker 31, page 97)

GENERAL ALFRED T. A. TORBERT

Born in Georgetown on July 1, 1833, Torbert attended local schools prior to his appointment to the West Point Class of 1855. After the out-break of the Civil War, he rose rapidly in rank, serving as a regimental and brigade commander of New Jersey troops, then as Commander of the 1st Cavalry Division of the Army of the Potomac, and finally as Commander of Cavalry, Army of the Shenandoah. He was breveted as Major General for his meritorious service. In 1869 Torbert was appointed by President Grant as Minister to San Salvador. He later served as Consul to Cuba and France. A shipwreck off the coast of Florida led to his death in 1880.

West Pine Street, north side, 1 1/2 blocks west of South Bedford Street, Georgetown. (S 96)

 GEORGE ALFRED TOWNSEND BIRTHPLACE

George Alfred Townsend, famous Civil War newspaper correspondent, journalist and author, was born on this block on January 30, 1841. Townsend's novels and poetry reflect his deep love for his native region. His best-known historical novel, *The Entailed Hat*, recounts the legend of Patty Cannon, the notorious slave runner of the Eastern Shore. In the late 1880's he designed and built "Gathland," his architecturally unique estate in the mountains west of Frederick, Maryland. His home is now a state park.

DE 9 near Georgetown Circle, Georgetown. (S 72)

31 GEORGETOWN

Site of town purchased May 9, 1791 from Abraham Harris, Rowland Bevins, and Joshua Pepper, and laid out for county seat of Sussex County in accordance with Act of General Assembly of January 29, 1791. Named Georgetown in honor of George Mitchell, for several sessions Speaker of State Senate and prominent member of commission appointed to lay out the town. Home of Governor Charles C. Stockley.

o *US 113 and DE 18, western edge of town, 0.9 mile from Georgetown Circle. (S 17)*

o *US 113 and US 9, east side, 0.8 mile from Georgetown Circle. (S 18)*

o *US 9, north side, 0.7 mile east of Georgetown Circle. (S 36)*

o *US 9 and Rd. 48, south side, one mile from Georgetown Circle. (S 46)*

 GEORGETOWN HUNDRED

First created 1833, by Act of General Assembly, which provided that Broadkill Hundred be divided into two hundreds, the eastern to be known as Broadkiln and the western as Georgetown. In 1835 this Act was repealed and Georgetown Hundred disappeared. It was recreated in 1861.

o *US 113, west side, eight miles north from Georgetown Circle. (S 16)*

o *US 113, east side, 4.4 miles south of Georgetown Circle. (S 19M)*

o *US 9, north side, 5.2 miles from Georgetown Circle. (S 37M)*

o *US 9, south side, 3.1 miles from Georgetown Circle. (S 41)*

o *DE 404, south side, 2.6 miles from Georgetown Circle. (S 47M)*

 GEORGETOWN PRESBYTERIAN CHURCH

In 1859 a petition was submitted to the Lewes Presbytery requesting the creation of a Presbyterian church in Georgetown. The congregation was organized the following year. Meetings were first held in the Sussex County Courthouse. The church was incorporated in 1871, and the present site was obtained for the construction of a house of worship. The new chapel was dedicated in December 1872.

The building was extensively renovated in 1934, when the church was raised and a basement level added. The structure was expanded in 1954 with the construction of a church school addition. A brick veneer exterior was added

WOODLAND FERRY

WOODLAND FERRY

NANTICOKE RIVER, AT WOODLAND FERRY

The **Woodland Ferry** (Cannon's Ferry) is the last cable operated ferry in Delaware. The ferry has been carrying passengers across the **Nanticoke River** since the late 18th century. (See marker 16, page 91)

at that time. A major expansion project was undertaken in 1999 with the addition of a Fellowship Hall and Christian Education facilities. The new wing was formally dedicated by the congregation in 2001.

203 North Bedford Street, Georgetown. (S 132)

34 GODWIN'S SCHOOL-DISTRICT # 190

On March 10, 1896, the State Board of Education approved a resolution recommending the creation of a new school district to serve the needs of local residents. The recommendation was forwarded to the Sussex County Levy Court with a petition from fifteen property owners stating that the neighborhood possessed more than the 35 "scholars" required to consider their request. The creation of District # 190 was formally approved the following June.

A subscription was circulated to raise funds to construct a school here on land provided by local store owner Jacob Reese Godwin. The new school was named in his honor. Classes were held here until 1936, when the district was consolidated with Millsboro School # 23.

South side of Rd. 20 at Rd. 410, 2 miles northwest of Millsboro. (S 129)

35 GOSHEN CEMETERY

In 1801 funds were raised to support the building of a place of worship for local Methodists. On January 16, 1802, church trustees purchased land here "on a rising ground beautifully situated for that purpose." A frame chapel was erected soon thereafter and given the name Goshen. The building remained in use until 1879, when a new church on Federal Street was completed. The old meeting house was sold the following year and moved to another location. Land where the building once stood became part of the cemetery.

On November 12, 1817, the Trustees of the Milton Academy purchased land on the west side of the church lot on which to build a school. For many years the academy enjoyed a distinguished reputation for scholastic excellence. It was closed circa 1880. In 1894 the academy lot was conveyed to the Public School Commissioners of Milton. A two-story frame building was then constructed on the site. Milton's first "High School" remained in use until 1933, when it was replaced by a new facility at another location.

Following the construction of the church a cemetery was established on the grounds. For many years it served as the chief burial place for the residents of the community. Growing concern about the maintenance of the property resulted in the formation of the Milton Cemetery Improvement Company in 1928. Responsibility for the cemetery was transferred to the corporation by the church. In 1966 the lot where the school buildings had stood was purchased for the cemetery expansion. Notable burials include those of David Hazzard, Governor of Delaware 1830-1833, and James Ponder, Governor of Delaware 1871-1875.

North side of Chestnut Street at Coulter Street, Milton. (S 127)

36 GOVERNOR JOHN COLLINS

Here stood Collins Forge, a bloomery iron works that smelted Sussex County bog iron from 1812 until 1850. Governor John Collins [1775-1821] and his son Theophilus, operators of the works, are buried nearby.

DE 18 across from Collins Pond, located between Rd. 42 and Rd. 527. (S 67)

37 GOVERNOR NATHANIEL MITCHELL

This Federalist served as the Governor of Delaware between 1805-1808. He was born in Laurel in 1752, attended Old Christ Church, and is buried in this churchyard. Mitchell was commissioned as Adjutant of Militia 1775, promoted captain in 1776, and appointed brigade major in 1779. He was a delegate to the Continental Congress between 1786-

The **Causey Mansion**, located in Milford, was purchased in 1850 by Peter Foster Causey. Causey was governor of Delaware from 1855 to 1859. He remodeled the house in Greek Revival style. It was previously the home of Governor Daniel Rogers. (Currently operates as a bed and breakfast)

1788 and was a member of Delaware's General Assembly between 1808-1812.

Willow Street and Delaware Avenue, Laurel. (S 68M)

GOVERNOR ROSS MANSION

This residence was constructed by William Henry Harrison Ross. He was born in Laurel in 1814 and died in 1887. He served as Governor of Delaware between 1851-1855. In 1859, Ross constructed this elaborate brick Italian Villa style structure featuring a three-story center entry tower on his 1,395 acre farm. Currently owned by the Seaford Historical Society, the property also includes a period barn, granary, and carriage house.

Rd. 543 near Rd. 534 intersection, across from the Seaford Industrial Park. (S 77)

39 GRACE UNITED METHODIST CHURCH

In 1827, a Methodist society was formed in this community, then known as Washington. On February 16, 1828, representatives of the congregation purchased a parcel of land for the purpose of erecting "a house or place of worship" for its members. The church became known as "Washington Methodist Episcopal Church." In 1874, the congregation erected a new church on its lot at the northwest corner of Main and Church Streets. This building was sold and moved in 1896. A new building was completed the following year, It was destroyed by fire in 1905. Another church was constructed and dedicated on December 16, 1906. This structure would later serve as Millsboro's post office and public library.

On December 18, 1928, the Trustees of the church, then known as "Grace Methodist Episcopal Church," purchased this site from the State Board of Education. It had previously been the location of the Millsboro Public School. Construction of the present church was commenced in 1949. The building was formally opened on October 8, 1950.

Southwest corner of Church and Morris Streets, Millsboro. (S 136)

40 GUMBORO HUNDRED

Created 1873 by Act of General Assembly from the southern parts of Broad Creek and Dagsboro Hundreds.

- o *DE 26 and Rd. 25, north of Rd. 413 intersection, west side, 7.1 miles south west from Millsboro. (S 57)*
- o *DE 26, east side, 13 miles from Millsboro at Maryland line. (S 58M)*

41 GUMBORO UNITED METHODIST CHURCH

Gumboro United Methodist Church traces its roots from the post Civil War era when a group of local citizens organized under the name of Union Methodist Episcopal Church. In the early 1870's the church purchased the structure used by the Gumboro Methodist Protestant Church for $350.00. The members of the M.P. Church subsequently joined this congregation. On March 17, 1881 the church incorporated as "Union Methodist Episcopal Church of Gumboro Hundred." A second incorporation took place on June 5, 1890 when the name was changed to "Gumboro M.E. Church." In 1924 David R. Baker donated the present site where a new church was erected and dedicated the following year.

One block east of DE 26, near Rd 413. and Rd. 17 intersection, Gumboro. (S 106)

HICKORY HILL METHODIST CHURCH

For many years local Methodists were forced to travel a considerable distance to attend services. In 1873, Houston's School House was established as a preaching place within the local circuit. The success of this effort stimulated interest in building a church. On September 11, 1877, Robert B. Houston conveyed an acre of land at this location for that purpose. Construction of Houston Methodist Episcopal Church was completed the following year. The church became the focus of community life, hosting traditional events such as Children's Day, Homecoming, and Christmas Entertainment. Outdoor services or "bush" meetings were

HIGHBALL SIGNAL, DELMAR

OLD CHRIST CHURCH, LAUREL

TREASURES OF THE SEA EXHIBIT, GEORGETOWN

INTERIOR, OLD CHRIST CHURCH

Highball Signal - In the 19th century, a red ball was pulled on a pole as a signal to the train engineer to stop. Next to the signal, a 1929 caboose serves as a museum for railroad artifacts dating from the 1800's. (See marker 43, page 103) The **Treasures of the Sea Exhibit** features artifacts recovered from a sunken Spanish galleon. The exhibit is located on the campus of the Delaware Technical and Community College, Georgetown. (See marker 24, page 93) The **Old Christ Church** was built in 1772 on land purchased by a levy of 80,000 pounds of tobacco. (See marker 69, page 113)

held nearby, bringing spiritual renewal to those in attendance. The church was renamed in 1955.

Approximately 2 miles west of Frankford, near the intersection of Rd. 82 and Rd. 407. (S 113)

43 HIGHBALL SIGNAL

Signals of this type were used on early railroads to control train movements. When the track was clear, the station agent would hoist the ball, permitting the train to proceed. The signal is listed in the National Register of Historic Places.

North Pennsylvania Avenue near DE 54, Delmar. (S 69)

44 INDIAN MISSION UNITED METHODIST CHURCH

In 1881 the Nanticoke Indian people constructed this church to provide a place to join for religious devotions. Known as "Johnson's Chapel," the church was affiliated with the Methodist Protestant denomination. On March 27, 1884, the land upon which the church had been built was conveyed by Jesse E. and Elizabeth Joseph to Trustees Samuel B. Norwood, Whittington Johnson, David P. Truitt, James H. Clark, Elisha Wright, William A. Johnson, and John W. Harmon.

The church was formally incorporated on May 23, 1915. In 1921 a new building was constructed and named Indian Mission M. P. Church. The Nanticoke people continue to hold their religious services here, and the church continues to provide cohesiveness for the Nanticoke to retain their native heritage and culture.

The oldest marked grave is that of Ann Johnson, who died October 7, 1885. Indian Mission United Methodist Church was listed in the National Register of Historic Places on April 26, 1979.

Rd. 22 and Rd. 48, near Fairmount. (S 122)

45 INDIAN RIVER HUNDRED

So named in 1706. This hundred together with Lewes and Rehoboth, Broadkill, and Cedar Creek Hundreds, formed what the early settlers called "Old Sussex."

o *North side of Indian River, on east side of DE 24, Millsboro. (SC 53)*
o *DE 24, west side, 12.4 miles from Millsboro. (S 54M)*

46 INDIAN RIVER LIFE-SAVING STATION

With the expansion of the nation's maritime commerce following the Civil War, the need for improved methods of assisting ships in distress was apparent. Built in 1876 by the United States Life-Saving Service, The Indian River Life-Saving Station was part of a network of similar facilities which were constructed along the Atlantic seaboard. In 1915, the Life-Saving Service and the Revenue Cutter Service were merged to form the modern-day United States Coast Guard. The Coast Guard continued to operate the Indian River Station until it was decommissioned following a devastating coastal storm in 1962. The property was later transferred to the State of Delaware. For a time the Station was utilized as a maintenance facility by the state's transportation and natural resources agencies. In 1997, the facility was extensively renovated and restored to its 1905 appearance. It is now operated by the Delaware Seashore Preservation Foundation in partnership with the State of Delaware.

The Indian River Life-Saving Station was listed in the National Register of Historic Places in 1976.

DE 1, three miles south of Dewey Beach. (S 148)

47 THE JUDGES

This home takes its name from the many judges who have lived in it. The Judges was built circa 1809 by Peter Robinson, who served as Secretary of State for Delaware under three governors and was appointed Associate Justice for Sussex County in 1832. Following his death in 1836, his

BROAD CREEK AT BETHEL

CAREY'S CAMP

GREENWOOD CHICKEN FARM

CAREY'S CAMP

The community of **Bethel** prospered as a shipbuilding center in the late 19th century, relying on the abundant forests along the Nanticoke River for virgin pine, oak and cypress. Many houses in Bethel were built by ship carpenters and sea captains. (See marker 10, page 89) The pictured **Greenwood Chicken Farm** is representative of the huge poultry industry in Delaware, which had its origins in Ocean View. (See marker 68, page 113) **Carey's Camp**, near Millsboro, is host to annual worship services for two weeks during the summer. (See marker 17, page 91)

daughter Mary and her husband Edward Wooten, who served as Associate Justice from 1847-87, occupied the house and made substantial renovations to it. Other members of the bench who have lived here include Chancellor David T. Marvel, Judge Henry C. Conrad, Judge Caleb M. Wright, and Judge Battle R. Robinson. In 1979 the home and adjacent law offices were listed in the National Register of Historic Places.

West Market and Front Streets, northwest corner, Georgetown. (S 111)

 KING'S UNITED METHODIST CHURCH

The origin of this congregation can be traced to the formation of a local society of the Methodist Episcopal Church in 1842. Known as the Oak Grove Society, the group held its first meetings in an old dwelling that was located approximately one-half mile south of here. Soon desiring a more suitable place of worship, funds were solicited and a church building was constructed at this location on land provided by William C. King. Completed in 1842, the church was named Hepburn to honor a subscriber to the building's construction.

By the 1880's the growth of the congregation and deteriorating condition of the first church resulted in an effort to build a new house of worship. Construction of the present church was commenced in the summer of 1884. A formal dedication service was held on January 4, 1885. As a result of a vote of its members, the name of the church was changed to King's as a tribute to the family that had given so generously since its founding.

A Community House was constructed in 1925. It was replaced by the present structure in 1949. Expansion of the nearby road led to the movement of the church in 1956. As a result, the building was extensively renovated and expanded to include the present Sunday School facility.

Southeast of Laurel, near intersection of Rd. 70 and Rd. 451. (S 134)

 LAUREL

Site of town was originally part of tract known as "Batchelor's Delight." From 1711 to 1768 it was included in Nanticoke Indian Reservation, comprising 3000 acres, authorized by Act of Maryland Assembly. A village known as Laurel was in existence as early as 1799. Home of Governors Mitchell, Cooper, and Marvil.

- o *US 13 and US 9, 13.7 miles from Georgetown Circle. (S 8M)*
- o *US 13A, southwest corner of High School Athletic Field, near 10th Street, 15.1 miles from Georgetown Circle. (S 11M)*

 LAUREL

This site was originally part of a tract known as "Bachelor's Delight." From 1711 to 1768 it was included in a 3,000 acre Nanticoke Indian Reservation, authorized by an Act of the Maryland Assembly. A village known as "Laurel" existed as early as 1799. Birthplace of Governor William H. H. Ross [elected 1850], and home to Governors Nathaniel Mitchell [elected 1804], William B. Cooper [elected 1840], Joshua H. Marvil [elected 1894], and Elbert N. Carvel [elected 1948 and 1960]. The town's central district was placed on the National Register of Historic Places in 1988.

US 13A and 10th Street, Laurel. (S 84)

51 LEWES

Under orders from Peter Stuyvesant, the Dutch erected fort at Hoorn Kil [Lewes Creek] 1659 but were soon dispossessed by the Marylanders. Here was also a communistic settlement established in 1662 by Mennonites from Holland under Peter Cornelis Plockhoy. Sir Robert Carr, 1664, "destroyed the quaking colony of Plockhoy to a naile."

US 9, south side, one mile west of Lewes Creek Bridge. (S 31)

GOVERNOR HAZZARD'S HOME, MILTON

ABBOTT'S MILL

ABBOTT'S MILL

ABBOTT'S MILL

Hazzard Home - Governor David Hazzard (born 1781 in Milton, died in 1864) was governor of Delaware from 1830 to 1833. His home is located at 327 Union Street, Milton. (Private residence, closed to the public) **Abbott's Mill**, located near Milford, is a historical property and Nature Center owned by the state and operated by the Delaware Nature Society. The center offers wholesome outdoor activities such as picnicking, hiking, bird watching, camping and boating (See marker 1, page 85)

52   LEWES

The Dutch in 1673 established a court at Hoorn Kil for the inhabitants "on the east and west sides of Cape Henlopen unto Bomties [Bombay] Hook." Governor Andros of New York 1676 established an English court at Whorekill, the jurisdiction of which was reduced 1681 by the creation of Kent County. County Seat of Sussex County until 1791.

US 9, north side, 0.8 mile from Lewes Creek Bridge. (SC 32)

 53   LEWES

Here lived Ryves Holt, Colonial Chief Justice; and four governors, David Hall, who commanded a Delaware regiment in the Revolution, Daniel Rodney and Caleb Rodney, sons of John Rodney, and Ebe W. Tunnell; also Colonel Henry Fisher, Revolutionary patriot, and Dr. Jacob Jones, later Commodore, U.S.N.

US 9, north side, 0.6 mile from Lewes Creek, on Lewes High School Grounds. (S 33)

 54   LEWES

On north side of town was Zwaanendael, first Dutch settlement on Delaware soil. Founded 1631 on creek, named by settlers Hoorn Kil in honor of town of Hoorn in Holland. Colony was destroyed by Indians same year. DeVries, a director of company which had sent out colony, came over the next year with aid but returned to Holland 1633.

US 9, south side on Zwaanendael House grounds. 0.1 mile from Lewes Creek Bridge. (S 34)

55   LEWES

Lewes was bombarded by British March 13, 1813, when Col. Samuel B. Davis, Commander of American Troops, refused a demand upon the people for fresh provisions. For many years Lewes was a Port of Call for ocean going vessels and

has been the home of many Delaware River pilots.

Lewes Creek Bridge, south side of State Street. (S 35M)

 56   LEWES AND REHOBOTH HUNDRED

Known as Rehoboth Hundred from 1698 onward. The name Lewes was added later. This hundred together with Indian River, Broadkill, and Cedar Creek Hundreds formed what the early settlers called "Old Sussex." Name, Lewes, comes from borough in Sussex County, England. Rehoboth is a Biblical name meaning spaces or places.

o   *US 1, west side, south of Red Mill Pond, 14.3 miles from Georgetown Circle. (S 30M)*
o   *US 9, south side, near Rd. 281, 8.5 miles from Georgetown Circle. (S 40)*
o   *DE 24, east side, 12.5 miles north of Millsboro. (S 55M)*

 57   LINE UNITED METHODIST CHURCH

On January 31, 1785, Planner Shores sold a one acre lot to the trustees of the local Methodist society. A part of a tract known as "Pleasant Grove," the land was located on the border of Delaware and Maryland. The deed stipulated that a preaching house or chapel be built "for the use of the Methodist preachers." Due to its unique location, the church became known as the Line Church. Bishop Francis Asbury ministered to congregations here on several occasions. The present building was constructed in 1874 to accommodate the growing congregation. In 1995 the church was designated as a Historic Site of the Peninsula-Delaware Annual Conference of the United Methodist Church.

North of DE 54 and Rd. 456 intersection, seven miles west of US 13 and DE 54 intersection, near Whitesville. (S 104)

 58   LITTLE CREEK HUNDRED

Originally claimed as part of Somerset County, Maryland. Upon confirmation of boundary lines between Maryland

The Masten House - This brick house was built in 1727 and enlarged to its present size in 1733. The house is one of the oldest brick structures in Sussex County. (The house is a private residence, not open to the public.) (See marker 60, page 109)

and Delaware in 1775, this hundred became part of Sussex County, Delaware.

- o *US 13, east side, south of Broad Creek, 14.1 miles from Georgetown Circle. (S 10)*
- o *US 13A and Jewell Street, 0.1 mile north of Delaware-Maryland Line, east side, Delmar. (S 12)*

 ### MARINER'S BETHEL UNITED METHODIST CHURCH

During the spring of 1779, Methodist pioneer Freeborn Garrettson visited this area to bring the message of his faith to the people. Garrettson's efforts were favorably received, and a number of local Methodist "societies" were organized. Among these was the Cedar Neck Society, and it is to this group that the origin of this church can be traced. While local "class meetings" were often held outside or in private residences, for many years members were forced to travel some distance to worship in a church.

On October 1, 1858, the society purchased a small lot of land at this location on which a church was to be constructed. The building was completed and dedicated the following year. The church became known as "Mariner's Bethel" in recognition of the occupation of many of its members. On June 16, 1894, four acres of adjoining land was purchased for the purposes of building a new church and expanding the cemetery. The new building was completed in 1899.

A Community Hall was added to the sanctuary in 1926, and then replaced with the construction of a new education building that was completed in 1959. The sanctuary's interior and exterior were completely renovated at that time. The Education Building was subsequently renovated during the time of construction of a new addition completed in 1995.
South side of Rd. 26 at Rd. 84, Ocean View. (S 124)

 ### MASTEN HOUSE

This brick house was built in 1727 and enlarged to its present size in 1733. It is one of the oldest brick structures in Sussex County. The Masten House is listed in the National Register of Historic Places.
Seaford-Atlantic Road [Rd. 30]. (S 70)

 ### MAULL HOUSE

This house is believed to have been built by Samuel Paynter, a carpenter who purchased this property in 1737. Following its completion, the house and surrounding land was sold in 1741 to Luke Shields, a prominent bay and river pilot. The close proximity of the bay and safe harbor of nearby Lewes Creek made this a prime location for those who practiced the competitive piloting profession. This section of Lewes, then some distance from the village, was known as Pilot Town, reflecting the occupation of its residents.

The property was purchased by Thomas S. Maull in 1836. The house was expanded with the addition of the present rear wing circa 1890, and it remained in the possession of the Maull family until 1957. It was obtained by the Colonel David Hall Chapter, National Society Daughters of the American Revolution, in 1962. The Maull House was listed in the National Register of Historic Places in 1970.
542 Pilot Town Road, Lewes. (S 138)

 ### MILFORD

Town laid out by Joseph Oliver 1787. Village was located on tract then called "Saw-Mill Range." Named Milford from fording place near mill-dam erected by Rev. Sydenham Thorne across Mispillion Creek, 1787. First incorporated 1807. Old town in Kent County, new town in Sussex County. Home of Governors Tharp, Causey, Burton, and Watson.

- o *US 113 at intersection with Shawnee Road, one mile from Front and Walnut Streets, Milford. (S 14)*
- o *Corner of Walnut and South-east Second Streets, Milford. (S 26M)*

The **Lewes-Rehoboth Canal** is an inlet waterway for pleasure craft and commercial vessels of small draft to go from the Delaware Bay into the Rehoboth and Indian River Bays.

MILTON

Located at the head of the Broadkill River, Milton became an important point for the shipping of agricultural products during the 18th century. A thriving shipbuilding industry supported the growth of the community, with large numbers of vessels being produced by local shipyards. Once known as Osborne's Landing and Head-of-the-Broadkill, the town was renamed Milton in 1807 and incorporated by the State Legislature on March 17, 1865.

o *DE 5 in front of school, Milton. (S 82)*
o *DE 5 and DE 16, Milton. (S 83)*

 MOUNT OLIVET UNITED METHODIST CHURCH

On February 9, 1830, a group of citizens favorable to the reform of the Methodist Episcopal Church joined together for the purpose of planning the establishment of a new church in Seaford. An existing meeting house standing on Chapel Branch was purchased the following day. The frame structure was then moved to the present site adjacent to the Hooper Burial Ground. Led by Dr. William Morgan, a physician and long-time local preacher, the new congregation affiliated themselves with the emerging Methodist Protestant denomination.

A new frame church was built in 1862. As a consequence of continued growth, the construction of the present brick building was initiated in 1897. The new church was dedicated on June 5, 1898. Numerous additions have been made since that time. In 1911 a pipe organ was added with a third of the cost being given by the famous industrialist and philanthropist, Andrew Carnegie.

In 1962 the sanctuary was remodeled and enlarged. The original stained glass was preserved in the new sanctuary. The chapel still retains much of its original appearance.

315 High Street, Seaford. (S 126)

 NANTICOKE HUNDRED

Named after Nanticoke Indian Tribe. This hundred, before 1775, was embraced in two hundreds, Deep Creek and Nanticoke, the latter including grants of land by Province of Maryland. When Mason and Dixon Line between Maryland and Delaware was confirmed, these hundreds were consolidated.

o *US 9, north side, 3.1 miles from Georgetown Circle. (S 42)*
o *US 9 and DE 20, south side, 7.3 miles from Georgetown Circle. (S 43M)*
o *DE 404, north side, 2.6 miles from Georgetown Circle. (S 48M)*
o *DE 404, south side, 10 miles from Georgetown Circle. (S 49M)*

 NANTICOKE POST NO. 6

In 1926 a group of local World War I veterans held a meeting in Burton's Hardware Store for the purpose of organizing an American Legion Post in Seaford. The initial effort was unsuccessful, but later that year plans were revived and the Nanticoke Post No. 6 received its charter. In 1934 members constructed the present Post home here on the former site of St. John's Methodist Episcopal Church. Church trustees had obtained the property in 1818 to serve as the site for "Bochim's Meeting House." Worship services were held here until the congregation relocated in 1898.

Nanticoke Post No. 6 was built in log cabin style with lumber hauled here by teams of horses. The fireplace was built of stone taken from the site of the 18th century Cape Henlopen Lighthouse. The Post was formally dedicated on June 6, 1953. In 1934, Post Commander Harry Truitt and Raymond E. Lloyd, Sr., obtained a 4.7" cannon from the Army's Aberdeen Proving Grounds for display at the Post. This 1908 model howitzer was one of 55 that were manufactured for training purposes prior to World War I. In 1952 an older artillery piece of unknown origin was donated

The **Zwaanendael Museum** features artifacts relating to the 1631 Dutch settlement at Lewes and the rich history of Sussex County. The building, built in 1931 to commemorate the first European settlement in Delaware, features an ornamental gable with carved stonework, and is an adaptation of the old town hall in Hoorn, Holland. (See marker 54, page 107)

for display. Its appearance is typical of British long guns that were used extensively in the last half of the 18th century.

West side of Front Street between Poplar and Third Streets, Seaford. (S 114)

 NORTHWEST FORK HUNDRED

Known by that since 1682, and originally embraced all territory west of Northwest Fork, a branch of Nanticoke River. Claimed by Maryland until Delaware obtained undisputed title in 1775, upon confirmation of Mason and Dixon Line. Seaford Hundred was detached 1869.

- o   *US 13, west side, at Sussex and Kent Counties line, 20.2 miles from Georgetown Circle. (SC 1)*
- o   *US 13, east side, 12.2 miles from Georgetown Circle. (S 2M)*
- o   *DE 404, north side, 10.5 miles from Georgetown Circle. (S 51M)*

 **OCEAN VIEW, DELAWARE
BIRTHPLACE OF THE COMMERCIAL BROILER INDUSTRY**

In 1923, Cecile Long Steele started a flock of 500 chicks. At 16 weeks, they weighted 2 1/4 pounds and sold for 62 cents a pound. By 1989, growers produced birds of twice the weight in half the time. Sussex County leads the nation in broiler production, now a multibillion dollar industry.

Ocean View Park off Central Avenue, Ocean View. (S 78)

 OLD CHRIST CHURCH

Established on Broad Creek in 1770 as a "Chapel of Ease" of Stepney Parish, Maryland on land purchased by a levy of 80,000 pounds of tobacco. Building completed by Robert Holston in 1772 at a cost of £ 510. Following the Revolutionary War this church was second of importance in the Diocese of Delaware.

DE 24 to Rd. 465 and Rd. 74, south of Chipman Pond, north side, two miles east of Laurel. (S 63)

 OLD COURTHOUSE

Constructed in 1791 at the direction of the State Legislature, this structure served as the seat of Sussex County government until 1837, when it was sold and moved to this location to make way for the construction of the present County Courthouse. It was later used as a private residence, and also served as a printing shop. On September 20, 1962, the building and lot were conveyed to the State of Delaware. A major renovation project was undertaken in 1974 with funding provided by the state and the National Park Service. The building was dedicated on Return Day in 1976, in honor of the Nation's Bicentennial.

South Bedford Street, west side, one-half block south of Public Circle, Georgetown. (S 91)

 OLD COURT HOUSE

In 1680, Governor Andros authorized the erection of a court house of logs to cost 5,000 pounds of tobacco. Near this wall was the second building, used from 1740 to 1791, when the county seat was removed to Georgetown. The church rented building as a tavern from 1797 to 1833, when it was razed and the ground included in the churchyard.

On wall enclosing churchyard of Saint Peter's Protestant Episcopal Church facing Third Street, Lewes. [Bronze Tablet]

 OLD SOUND METHODIST CHURCH

In April, 1779, one of the state's first Methodist societies was organized near this site by Reverend Freeborn Garrettson. On April 29, 1784, one acre of ground was purchased here for the erection of a "preaching house." The church became known as Williams Chapel, in honor of brothers Arthur and Ezekiel Williams, founding members and prominent local preachers. Services were conducted here until the congregation relocated to a nearby site purchased in 1871. The church building was moved from this location at that

HIRAM R. BURTON HOUSE, LEWES HISTORICAL SOCIETY

RABBIT'S FERRY HOUSE, LEWES HISTORICAL SOCIETY

THOMPSON COUNTRY STORE, LEWES HISTORICAL SOCIETY

The **Lewes Historical Society Complex**, beginning at the corner of Third and Shipcarpenter Streets, features historical homes and businesses. The **Hiram R. Burton House** (c. 1780), the **Rabbit's Ferry House** and the **Thompson Country Store** are part of the complex.

time. On December 7, 1896, the Trustees of the Church conveyed the property to Charles W. Johnson and Eliza J. Williams, for use as a cemetery.

DE 382A, north side, near intersection of Rd 382, Johnson. (S 92)

73 "PETTIJOHN'S OLD FIELD"

The future home of Sussex County's seat of government was a sparsely populated rural area when the 76 acres which would become the town of Georgetown were purchased on May 9, 1791. Located "near the centre" of the county at a place known as "James Pettijohn's Old Field," the land was surveyed by Rhoads Shankland, who divided it into lots which were sold to defray costs associated with the establishment of the town. The most prominent feature of his design was this public square, known today as The Circle.

Public Circle, northeast corner, Georgetown. (S 86)

74 PILOT TOWN

Pilot Town is the section of the hamlet of Concord where many free African-American families have lived in harmony with the white families since around 1765. It was so named for the many black pilots who lived in the area and piloted vessels down the Nanticoke River to Chesapeake Bay. Two of the best known were Cann Laws and George Laws.

DE 20 and DE 20A, north side, two miles west of US 13 and DE 20 intersection. (S 66)

75 PRINCE GEORGE'S CHAPEL

Before the settlement of the boundary dispute between Delaware and Maryland, this area was considered to lie in Maryland. On July 5, 1755, responding to the request of members of the Church of England residing in the upper portion of Worcester Parish, the Maryland Assembly enacted legislation authorizing the purchase of land and construction of a "Chapel of Ease" to serve their spiritual needs. A two acre tract at this location was then purchased from Walter Evans. On June 30, 1757, the newly-completed chapel was formally received from the builders by the vestry of Worcester Parish. It was named to honor the English prince who would become King George III.

By 1850 the condition of the chapel had deteriorated, and services were discontinued. Efforts to restore the church to active use were unsuccessful. Annual services were held here for a time, but for many years the building was maintained solely as a historic site by the Episcopal Diocese of Delaware. In 1928 the Sussex County Layman's League funded the complete restoration of the old church, and a rededication service was held here on June 30, 1929.

At the urging of numerous persons concerned about the preservation of the structure, the State of Delaware received ownership of the property in 1967. Major renovations were subsequently undertaken with funding provided by the State and National Park Service. Prince George's Chapel was listed in the National Register of Historic Places on March 24, 1971. Of particular note is the grave of General John Dagworthy, an officer in the French & Indian and Revolutionary Wars who was an early and ardent supporter of the church, and for whom this community is named.

North side of DE 26, near DE 26 and Rd. 302, Dagsboro. (S 118)

76 PROSPECT A.M.E. CHURCH

The roots of African-American Methodism in this community can be traced to the organization of a black "class" within the local Methodist society in the 1790's. By the 1830's a group of residents had affiliated themselves with Bishop Richard Allen's African Methodist Episcopal Church. On November 13, 1839, Trustees Moses Robinson, Timothy Jacobs, Curtis Jacobs, George Ratcliff, and Isaac Waples, purchased land for the construction of a church and establishment of a

BAILEY ART WEST HOUSE, LEWES

HARVARD HOUSE, LEWES

ORIGINAL METHODIST MEETING HOUSE, LEWES

Lewes is essentially a seafaring town with its excellent harbor, inlet canal to Rehoboth Bay, large fleet of charter fishing boats, and ferry to New Jersey. Lewes is also a walking town with museums, historic sites, antique shops, boutiques, convenient lodging, eateries and charming streets all within a short distance of each other.

cemetery. The original structure was replaced by the present church circa 1867. For many years Prospect A.M.E. was the site of one of the few schools for African-American youths in Sussex County.

West Railroad Street and Adams Street, two blocks south of East Market Street, Georgetown. (S 107)

77   PROVIDENCE METHODIST CHURCH

In 1865 the Maryland Conference of the Methodist Protestant Church established a "mission" or charge circuit in Sussex County. At the time local members of that faith were meeting nearby in Rogers School. Services were held in the schoolhouse until 1886, when the present church was built on land that had been provided by Harrison Rogers. The church lot was formally transferred to the trustees by Charles H. Elliott in 1924.

Following the closure of Rogers School in 1932, the congregation acquired the vacant building for use as a Community Hall. Constructed in 1904 to replace the earlier structure where the congregation had once met, the building was moved to its present location in 1933.

East side Rd. 431, 2.5 miles south of Rd. 431 and US 113, near Georgetown. (S 130)

78   QUEEN ANNE'S RAILROAD

In February 1895, the Delaware Legislature authorized the Queen Anne's Railroad, a Maryland corporation formed the previous year, to extend its lines across the state to Lewes. Their goal was to establish a direct link between Baltimore and the coast. The western terminus was at Queenstown, Maryland, with connections from there to Baltimore via steamship. The eastern terminus provided travelers with access to the Rehoboth resort via rail, and steamship connection with Cape May, New Jersey. This was the last major railroad built on the Delmarva peninsula.

Over forty years had passed since the first of several unsuccessful efforts to bring a railway to Milton. On August 29, 1897, the first passenger train arrived here, to be greeted by a majority of the residents of the town and surrounding countryside. A station was erected on this site in October of that year. Regular passenger and mail service was provided, and a wide variety of freight was shipped and received. For many years Milton was noted for the export of holly and other seasonal greenery to northern cities.

In 1905 the Queen Anne's Railroad was purchased by a subsidiary of the Pennsylvania Railroad. By the mid-1920's limited profits and competition with other lines owned by the company led to the decision to abandon a large portion of the old railway. Facing that prospect, the Denton to Lewes section was purchased by the Maryland & Delaware Coast Railway. This effort proved to be largely unsuccessful, and passenger service was discontinued in October 1931. Once again slated for abandonment, the Ellendale to Milton line was purchased in 1934 for the purpose of continuing a freight link to the town via rail. It would become the last significant operable section of the old Queen Anne's Railroad.

North side of Chestnut Street, east side of railroad, Milton. (S 116)

79   RELOCATION OF THE COUNTY SEAT

The conflicting claims of the proprietors of Maryland and Pennsylvania resulted in a lengthy and sometimes violent dispute concerning the ownership and boundaries of Sussex County. Residents who had been Marylanders before the controversy was resolved in 1775, found themselves to be inconvenienced when traveling to Lewes, the original seat of government. Hundreds of persons signed petitions requesting removal of the county seat to a more central location. On January 29, 1791, the Delaware Assembly approved legislation resulting in the establishment of Georgetown.

Public Circle, northwest corner, Georgetown. (S 88)

INDIAN RIVER INLET

INTERIOR, LIFESAVING STATION MUSEUM

LIFESAVING STATION MUSEUM

The **Indian River Inlet** connects the Atlantic Ocean with the Indian River Bay and Rehoboth Bay. The **Indian River Lifesaving Station Museum** is one of the few restored Lifesaving Stations on the East Coast. Built in 1876, "surfmen" drilled and worked here, rescuing sailors and passengers in distress. (See marker 46, page 103)

80   RETURN DAY

This event draws thousands as winning and losing candidates join in celebration on the Thursday following each general election. Poor traveling conditions and interest in the outcome of political contests may have resulted in an extended stay when all elections were held here. Creation of voting districts in 1811 required the meeting of a Board of Canvass on Thursdays to determine "returns" for the county. Proclamation of results continues to highlight this festive occasion. Well-established by the mid-19th century, Return Day is recognized as the only event of its kind in the nation.

Public Circle, southwest corner, Georgetown. (S 85)

81   RYVES HOLT

In this house lived Ryves Holt, Chief Justice of "Three Lower Counties on Delaware," 1745 to 1763; member of Assembly of "Three Lower Counties on Delaware," 1734-1737, 1742-1744, 1746-1755 and Speaker of Assembly, 1742-1744, and 1746-1752. Ryves Holt was probably born in 1696 and died in 1763.

House standing at south-west corner of Third and Mulberry Streets, Lewes. [Bronze Tablet]

82   SALEM UNITED METHODIST CHURCH

The origin of this church can be traced to the organization of a local Methodist society soon after the American Revolution. By 1790 the Sandy Branch Society was joining regularly for worship, holding services in the open air and in the homes of members. Some time thereafter the congregation constructed their first church at a location on the north side of present-day Selbyville. The building was also used as a school. Land where the structure stood was conveyed to church trustees in 1833. The first church was used until a new building was constructed near the old one on a lot of ground purchased in 1849.

The growth of the town and the prosperity of the congregation resulted in the desire for a new facility. In 1884 a new building was completed at the present site. This structure remained in use until 1911, when it was moved to an adjoining lot where a school had formerly stood. For a time the old building was also used for school purposes. It was destroyed by fire in 1922.

Construction of the present church was commenced in 1911 following the relocation of the older structure. A new parsonage was constructed as well. Total cost of the church and parsonage was approximately $ 25,000. Completion of the project was celebrated at a dedication service on July 14, 1912.

Northeast corner of Church Street and Church Avenue, Selbyville. (S 128)

83   SEAFORD

Town laid out, 1799. Then called "Hooper's Landing." First incorporated 1865. Seaford Academy located here from 1819 until some time before Civil War. Rev. Leonidas Polk, later Episcopal Bishop and Major General in Confederate Army was student at Academy. Home of William H. Ross, thirty-seventh Governor of Delaware.

o   *US 13A, west side, at northern entrance of Seaford. (S 4)*
o   *US 13 and Rd. 535, east side, south of Nanticoke River. (S 5)*

84   SEAFORD HUNDRED

Detached from Northwest Fork Hundred by Act of General Assembly, 1869. Northwest Fork Hundred, originally claimed by Maryland, then embraced all territory west of Northwest Fork. Delaware obtained undisputed title in 1775, upon confirmation of Mason and Dixon Line.

o   *US 13, west side, 12.2 miles from Georgetown Circle. (S 3M)*

Cape Henlopen Inner Breakwater Lighthouse was removed from service in 1994. It is now preserved as an historic landmark.

o DE 404 and Rd. 533,, south side, 10.5 miles from Georgetown Circle. (S 50)

o US 13A, west side, north of Nanticoke River, 15.2 miles from Georgetown Circle. (S 6)

 SHIPWRECK OF "THE FAITHFUL STEWARD"
September 2, 1785

Bound from Londonderry, Ireland to Philadelphia with 249 immigrants, "The Faithful Steward" ran aground on a shoal where she was destroyed by stormy seas with heavy loss of life.

DE 1 at Haven Road, oceanside, north of the Indian River Inlet Bridge. (S 73)

 SITE OF JACOBS SCHOOL # 143

In 1863 the Sussex County Levy Court formally approved the creation of a new school district to serve the needs of local citizens. A frame schoolhouse was constructed on this site on land provided by Thomas Jacobs. Measuring twenty feet in width and thirty-two feet in length, this was a one-room school with a single teacher who was responsible for teaching all students in grades 1-6. Classes were conducted at this location until 1917, when road improvements led to the movement of the building to a site one-third mile to the northwest. The school was then expanded and renovated. Jacobs School # 143 was closed following the consolidation of the district with Bridgeville District # 90 in 1929.

North side of Rd. 404, 0.4 miles east of Rd. 404 and US 13, near Bridgeville. (S 131)

 SLAUGHTER NECK UNITED METHODIST CHURCH

The history of this congregation can be traced to the early days of Methodism in this country. In 1777 a group of area residents gathered at the home of a "Mr. Shockley" to organize a local Methodist "society." While visiting in July 1779, Methodist pioneer Francis Asbury noted the rapid growth of the congregation and the enthusiasm of its members. For many years meetings were held outdoors and in private residences. On July 26, 1810, members gathered to elect trustees and organize themselves into a corporate body. The following October the trustees received a deed from local preacher William Hickman for land on which "Hickman's Meeting House" or "Zion" had been built.

In 1855 the congregation of "Zion Methodist Episcopal Church" purchased a one acre parcel adjoining the old church lot from Lemuel Draper, upon which a new church was built the following year. The building was enlarged and extensively renovated in 1888. It is believed that the stained glass windows in the present church were obtained at that time. The name of the church was changed to better reflect the community which it served. In 1928 concerns about the condition of the structure prompted members to undertake the construction of the present church. A service commemorating the laying of the cornerstone was held on November 24, 1929.

This marker was dedicated in memory of Doris Clifton Argo, Church Historian and Life Member of Slaughter Neck United Methodist Church-Homecoming 1997.

US 1 and DE 14, south of Argo's Corner. (S 115)

 ST. GEORGE'S METHODIST CHURCH

The roots of this church can be traced to the efforts of Reverend Elijah Hitch, a local preacher of the Methodist Episcopal denomination, who was invited by area residents to hold services in their homes during the spring of 1842. Later meetings were conducted at the local school, and a successful camp meeting was held nearby in July of that year. Desiring a more permanent place of worship, the new congregation purchased a half-acre of ground at this location on September 27, 1842. A church was then constructed. It

CAPE MAY-LEWES FERRY

RIVER PILOTS HOUSE

LEWES-REHOBOTH CANAL

The **Cape May-Lewes Ferry** makes a seventy-minute cruise across open salt water and is a perfect day trip from Lewes to Cape May, New Jersey resorts. The **River Pilots House** represents the starting point for ocean going vessels navigating up the Delaware River to inland ports. The **Lewes-Rehoboth Canal** offers the opportunity for a scenic inland pleasure boat trip from Lewes to Rehoboth Bay.

was named for one of the oldest Methodist churches in this country, St. George's in Philadelphia.

The first building was used until 1888, when the present church was constructed. A Community Hall was added in 1924. The Sunday School addition, which connects the two buildings, was completed in the 1950's.

West side of Rd. 501, 3.5 miles south of Laurel. (S 135)

 ST. GEORGE'S UNITED METHODIST CHURCH

The roots of this congregation can be traced to the late 1700's, when Methodist pioneers such as Francis Asbury and Freeborn Garrettson visited this area to propagate the faith . Meetings were held in the open air and in the private residences. By 1816 a group of local residents were joining together in worship. In 1833 land was purchased approximately one mile north of here for the construction of a church. Services were held there until 1880, when the present church was erected on land purchased from John Steele. The new building was formally dedicated on December 12, 1880. A major renovation and expansion of the church was undertaken.

DE 26 and Rd. 365, Clarksville. (S 109)

90 **ST. JOHN'S METHODIST CHURCH**

The origin of this congregation can be traced to the organization of "Johnson's Society" in the 1830's. Meetings were held in private homes and the local school. On July 3, 1852, trustees were elected to supervise the building of the first church. A one acre portion of the "Springfield" tract was subsequently purchased from James E. and Mary A. Blizzard. Construction was completed in 1853. The original structure was replaced by the present church in 1907. In 1950 a building was moved here from the site of the Civilian Conservation Corps Camp near Georgetown, for renovation and use as a church hall. St. John's was listed in the

National Register of Historic Places in 1990.

DE 30 and Rd. 47, 2.3 miles south of Gravel Hill, Springfield Crossroads. (S 108)

 ST. PAUL'S PROTESTANT EPISCOPAL CHURCH

Incorporated on June 21, 1794, St. Paul's P.E. Church is the oldest organized church in Georgetown. Prior to completion of the first church building, services were held in the Sussex County Courthouse. In 1805, a special lottery sanctioned by the State General Assembly raised $1,500 for construction of the first church. During the early 1840's, a brick structure replaced the original frame church. In 1880-81, the church was remodeled in the early Victorian Gothic style-the plans being attributed to McKim, Meade, and White, a New York architectural firm distinguished for planning a number of famous churches. St. Paul's P.E. Church was placed on the National Register of Historic Places in 1979.

East Pine and Academy Streets, Georgetown. (S 101)

 ST. PAUL'S UNITED METHODIST CHURCH

In 1865 the Maryland Conference of the Methodist Protestant Church established a "mission" or charge circuit in southwestern Sussex County. At the time local members of the faith were holding meetings in Sharp's School, a one room school house located less than one half mile from here. On August 21, 1868, the "Trustees of the Missionary Society of the M. P. Church" purchased land at this site from Thomas L. Cannon, on which the church was constructed. The building was completed and dedicated in 1871 by the Rev. W. D. Litsinger.

The church was formally incorporated as "St. Paul's Methodist Protestant Church" in 1897. A Community House was constructed in 1924. Two rooms connecting the church and Community House were added in 1951, and four Sunday School rooms were completed in 1964.

East side Rd. 68, one mile south of Rd. 68 and Rd. 70, near Laurel. (S 120)

DELAWARE SEASHORE STATE PARK

CAPE HENLOPEN STATE PARK

DELAWARE SEASHORE STATE PARK

CAPE HENLOPEN STATE PARK

Fort Miles Towers - Eleven concrete fire control towers, (known locally as submarine towers) were built sixty years ago along the Delaware coast from Cape Henlopen down to Fenwick Island. Many were part of the military installation named Fort Miles, created in 1941 on 1,000 acres of what is now Cape Henlopen State Park. Servicemen used the towers to scan the waters for any menacing warships on the Delaware Bay. The fort was decommissioned in 1959.

93 SUDLER HOUSE

Erected about 1750, with additions during the Federal Period. Land was granted to Cacilius Stevens in 1658. Francis Asbury preached here. William Jessop, an early occupant, was a pioneer Methodist missionary in Canada. From 1833 to 1971 the Sudler family owned the property.

US 13A, Main Street, Bridgeville. (S 71)

94 SUSSEX COUNTY COURTHOUSE

In 1835 a lottery was authorized to raise funds to replace the frame structure which had served as courthouse since 1791. Construction of the new building began in 1837 following the sale and relocation of the original courthouse to its present site on South Bedford Street. The Brick Hotel across the square was designated as the temporary seat of justice. Completed in 1839, the new courthouse was designed by nationally known architect William Strickland, and constructed by Layton & Sipple. A major renovation and expansion project was completed in 1969.

Public Circle, southwest corner, Georgetown. (S 87)

95 TOWN OF DELMAR

The town of Delmar was established soon after the Delaware Railroad reached this area in 1859. Although fire devastated Delmar in 1892 and 1901, the town continued to build and grow. Incorporated on March 9, 1899, Delmar became known as the "strawberry capital of the nation" in the early twentieth century due to the abundance of strawberries grown and shipped by farmers in the area. Located on the Mason-Dixon Line, Delmar took its name from the combination of the first three letters of both Delaware and Maryland. Because of Delmar's unique geographic situation, the town adopted the motto of "The Little Town Too Big To Be In One State."

East State and 6th Streets, Delmar. (S 103)

96 TRANSPENINSULAR LINE

This stone monument, erected April 26, 1751, marks the eastern end of the Transpeninsular Line surveyed 1750-1751 by John Watson and William Parsons of Pennsylvania and John Emory and Thomas Jones of Maryland. This line established the east-west boundary between Pennsylvania's "Three Lower Counties" [now Delaware] and the colony of Maryland. It established also the middle point of the peninsula, 35 miles to the west. The stone bears the coat of arms of the Calverts on the south side and the Penns on the north. It was accepted 1760 and finally ratified 1769 by King George III.

DE 54 at the Lighthouse, just off DE 1. (S 74)

97 UNION WESLEY UNITED METHODIST CHURCH AND CAMPGROUND

The roots of African-American Methodism in this area can be traced to the late 18th century when Methodist pioneers such as Francis Asbury and Freeborn Garrettson traveled locally organizing black "classes" for worship. Over time some groups chose to leave the mother church, while others such as this congregation remained affiliated with the Methodist Episcopal faith. By the mid-1800's members of Union Wesley were gathering regularly for services. Many of the early meetings were conducted in the open air nearby.

On December 18. 1873, the Trustees of Union Wesley purchased the lot where the first church was built. Standing in the area where the cemetery is located, the building served the needs of the congregation until it was destroyed by fire in 1957. The present church was erected here on the former site of the District #207-C Blackwater School. The land had been obtained in 1951 following the destruction of the school by fire. The new church was completed in 1961.

Prior to the placement of permanent structures on the Wesley Campground, persons attending services used

REHOBOTH BEACH

BETHANY BEACH

FENWICK ISLAND

DEWEY BEACH

Delaware's Atlantic Coastline offers twenty-five miles of outdoor pleasures and family enjoyment year round. Memorial Day weekend though Labor Day is peak season, but the spring and fall months are also popular for getaway weekends.

covered wagons for shelter. The wagons were placed in a circle surrounding a pulpit. By the 1930's wooden boarding "tents" had replaced the wagons, and a confectionery and bower had been constructed. One building that was adapted for use was the old #207-C Schoolhouse. Constructed in the late 19th century, the structure was used as a school until 1922, when it was replaced by the building that stood on this site. This was the last camp in Delaware to use wooden firestands for lighting purposes. Their use was discontinued in 1943 when electricity was brought to the grounds. Wesley Campground is believed to be one of the oldest of its type in continuous use.

East side of Rd. 365, 0.5 miles south of DE 26 and Rd. 365, Clarksville. (S 119)

98 WESLEY UNITED METHODIST CHURCH

This congregation's beginnings can be traced to a visit from Methodist pioneer Francis Asbury to a gathering of farm families at the home of Abraham Harris on September 24, 1779. A prominent local landowner, Mr. Harris later conveyed a substantial portion of the land upon which the town of Georgetown was built. For many years this local Methodist "society" met in the homes of its members. In April 1802, the congregation purchased a lot of land on West Pine Street, just east of South Lane, where a frame house of worship known as "Wesley Chapel" was erected. After fire destroyed this structure, a second building was constructed nearby on land purchased in 1806 from John Russell. This site is now part of the "old Methodist cemetery."

On July 9, 1859, the growing congregation purchased a lot of land on North Race Street, south of Cooper Alley, for the site of a new church. The building was completed and dedicated in 1865. By the 1890's, it was very evident that a larger sanctuary was needed. Under the leadership of the Rev. Charles A. Grise, the lot where the present church stands was purchased in 1896. Construction of the modified-Gothic design building was completed the following year. Church treasurer William J. McNatt served as supervising architect, and John Barr was the contractor. A formal dedication service was held on March 7, 1897.

The adjoining parsonage was built in 1907. The Willie M. Jones Memorial Hall was constructed in 1928, and the Education Building in 1956-57.

East side North Race Street between East Laurel Street and Cooper Alley, Georgetown. (S 117)

 ## 99 WESTWOODS METHODIST CHURCH

During the spring of 1779, Methodist pioneer Freeborn Garrettson visited this area to bring the message of his faith to the people. The efforts of Reverend Garrettson and others who followed were met with considerable success. Numerous "societies" or "classes" were organized as a result. Meetings were often held in private residences, there being considerable distance to travel to the nearest organized church.

Around 1880 a group of local residences began to hold services in the Good Hope School House. Soon after, they started to conduct "woods" or "bush" meetings in the open air nearby. A camp meeting ground was subsequently constructed. In 1892, on one day alone, fifty-eight youth were baptized at Westwoods Camp. While meetings were well attended, they were discontinued in the mid-1890's when the services were merged with those that were being held at other churches nearby.

In 1890 the congregation began the construction of a church. On March 23, 1891, trustees were elected, and the land where the church was built was conveyed to them by Joshua G. West. The building was completed later that year. The church was affiliated with the Gumboro Circuit of the Methodist Episcopal denomination. It was given the name Westwoods to reflect its wooded surroundings, and to honor

FENWICK ISLAND LIGHTHOUSE

TRANSPENINSULAR LINE MARKER, FENWICK ISLAND

The **Fenwick Island Lighthouse** began operation August 1859 and remained in operation until 1978. In 1981, public outcry led to reinstallation of the original light. The **Transpeninsular Line Marker** was erected in April 1751 and marks the east end of the southern boundary between Pennsylvania's Three Lower Counties (now Delaware) and Maryland. (See marker 96, page 125)

Joshua G. West and the other members of his family who had been instrumental in its creation and growth.

North side Rd. 426, 0.8 miles west of Rd. 426 and Rd. 26, near Gumboro. (S 121)

 WILLIAM C. JASON COMPREHENSIVE HIGH SCHOOL

First African-American Secondary School in Sussex County

Named after the first African-American President of Delaware State College, the school opened in October, 1950. Funds were provided in the will of H. Fletcher Brown, a local philanthropist, and by the State General Assembly. Initially Jason High School served grades 9 through 12, but in 1953 it expanded to include students from seventh and eighth grades. The desegregation of schools in Delaware led to the closing of Jason in June, 1967 after which it became part of Delaware Technical and Community College.

DE 18 and US 113, Georgetown. (S 80)

 ZOAR METHODIST CHURCH

Zoar Methodist Church was founded in the late 18th century. Bishops Coke and Asbury are believed to have ministered to congregations in a log structure which served as the first church building. A cypress-shingle church was constructed after the land was purchased from Robert and Sukey Lacey in 1802. Within a few years, camp meetings were held in the adjoining grove. The church was incorporated on November 5, 1810. Following a fire in 1910, the present structure was built. Much of the carpentry and masonry was completed by Rev. James L. Derrickson, pastor of the church. The last camp meeting was held in 1919. Annual homecoming services are held in late October.

DE 30 and Rd. 48, southeast corner, five miles south of US 9 and DE 30 intersection, Zoar. (S 99)

DELAWARE MEMORIAL BRIDGE

WILMINGTON, BRANDYWINE RIVER

NEMOURS MANSION

WINTERTHUR POINT TO POINT STEEPLECHASE RACES

The easiest way to begin exploring the wonders of Delaware is to get off the Delaware Turnpike (I-95) which cuts through New Castle County. A good place to start your journey is Wilmington, Delaware's largest city. If you continue north of Wilmington, you will come to the amazing house and gardens of Nemours Mansion, and slightly beyond that you will find the equally dazzling house and gardens of Winterthur.

DELAWARE TODAY
NEW CASTLE COUNTY

First-time visitors to New Castle County say very often, "The history - the lovely villages, towns and museums - the mansions and gardens - fountains, theatres and concert halls - fabulous art - the Brandywine River and gorgeous countryside! We didn't know you had anything like this - and so much of it, too! We'll be back."

From its early days as a colonial outpost in the New World, it has moved through times of fur trading and agriculture; to water-powered mills producing world-famous flour, paper and gunpowder; to ship and railroad car building; to the modern chemical industry and high tech banking. New Castle County offers visitors and residents countless opportunities to learn its history, enjoy its many present-day amenities, and partake in the shaping of its future.

The New Castle County of today is a unique blend of urban and rural communities. Small towns like Odessa and Middletown in the south of the county, and Arden near the Pennsylvania border to the north, still exhibit a more serene and simple way of life. Newark, on the western border has a culture all its own as the home of the University of Delaware (one of 6 colleges with a campus in New Castle County). At the opposite end of the spectrum is Wilmington, Delaware's largest city and undisputed center of technology and commerce. The wonderful thing about this diversity is that residents and visitors can easily enjoy both. Stay in a small- town bed & breakfast and visit Wilmington for what the city offers, or stay in a world-class hotel in Wilmington and daytrip out to the surrounding countryside.

It is hard to talk about contemporary New Castle County without recognizing its past. Names such as du Pont have been a part of the area from the beginning and are still a driving force today. New Castle County is proud of the many historical attractions it offers, most of which have been noted by the historical marker program. There are far too many to list here, but a few which should not be missed are the du Pont estates of Winterthur and Nemours, the Hagley Museum, Historic Houses of Odessa, Fort Delaware State Park, and the historic 18th century charm of the city of New Castle. Many attractions allow an interactive experience with the past such as a sail tour aboard the ship Kalmar Nyckel or a ride on the steam-powered train of the Wilmington and Western Railroad. Still other sites have reclaimed historic buildings and are in full use today like the Grand Opera House and the Hotel du Pont in Wilmington.

Not far from these historic sites near Rodney Square are beautiful office buildings built by DuPont, Wilmington Trust, MBNA, Chase, PNC, Hercules, and others. Wilmington has become a commerce center recognized worldwide. As the centerpiece of New Castle County, the city offers travelers and residents the best in amenities, transportation, education and recreation. New and restored first-class and boutique hotels delight visitors. Wonderful shops with apartments and lofts above can be found in the historic Ships Tavern District. A new Justice Center with over 50 courtrooms has been constructed on Rodney Square. The busy center of downtown activity is spreading over an ever-larger area. On the Christina Riverfront, the Transportation Center and restored Amtrak Station (the nation's ninth busiest with over 80 trains daily) provide easy access to and from points beyond. The Wilmington Youth Rowing Association puts hundreds of young people on the river in 1, 2 and 8-person shells. There is also the Tubman-Garrett Riverfront Park and a beautiful 1.2-mile Riverwalk, complete with 21 colorful historic panels. The Riverwalk runs upstream to the Riverfront Market and ING Direct, past the Delaware Theatre Company, the Backstage Café, the Delaware Center for the Contemporary Arts, Kahunaville, and on to Frawley Stadium (home of the Wilmington Blue Rocks minor league baseball team), the FirstUSA Riverfront Arts Center (art and history exhibitions), and the Shipyard Shops (outlet stores). With the revitalization of the Riverfront visitors can enjoy good restaurants, acclaimed international exhibitions, lively concerts, and tax-free shopping.

If the Riverwalk leaves you wanting more outdoor activity, there are plenty of choices in New Castle County. State parks and other recreation areas offer hiking, camping, biking and more. At Brandywine State Park you can canoe or go tubing on the Brandywine River. Swim, fish and boat on the state's largest freshwater pond at Lums Pond State Park (and if you don't have a boat, you can rent one!). Horse riding trails as well as hiking are available at historic Bellevue State Park. Whatever your interest, there is certainly something for everyone to see, do and enjoy.

This is New Castle County, Greater Wilmington and the Brandywine Valley! Still historic - how amazing!

KALMAR NYCKEL ON THE CHRISTINA RIVER

CHRISTINA RIVER-WILMINGTON

WILMINGTON & WESTERN RAILROAD

PORT OF WILMINGTON

New Castle County is the northern-most county in Delaware. The Christina River which flows along the south side of Wilmington has become the focus of a growing recreation, arts and shopping complex. The Wilmington & Western Railroad was once an important part of the local economy. Traveling through scenic countryside, it allows passengers to experience transportation from the golden days of steam-powered engines.

WINTERTHUR GARDENS

NEMOURS MANSION

DELAWARE MEMORIAL BRIDGE

BRANDYWINE VALLEY

Some of the wonders of New Castle County continue north of Wilmington along the Brandywine River. For years the mills along the Brandywine River have been a source of considerable wealth. This wealth was responsible for the great gardens and mansions in the area such as Winterthur and Nemours.

DELAWARE AGRICULTURE MUSEUM

DOVER DOWNS HARNESS RACING

DOVER DOWNS - THE GAMES

DOVER AIR FORCE BASE MUSEUM

Kent County is best known for being the home of Dover, the state capital, as well as Dover Air Force Base. Dover is also known for Dover Downs which hosts NASCAR racing, harness racing and slot machines, all of which bring in huge crowds of visitors to Kent County.

DELAWARE TODAY
KENT COUNTY

Kent County is the center of the three counties comprising Delaware. Though deeply rooted in the past, the Kent County of today has much to offer its residents and visitors. It is a unique place where the past exists with today, while allowing today to progress and grow to tomorrow.

Featuring fertile soil and a temperate climate, agriculture has long supported the local economy, and throughout the 19th century and into the 20th, most of the inhabitants of Kent County engaged in farming for their livelihood. As technological advances came to the farming industry, this began to change. The building of Dover Air Force Base ushered in a new era of modern corporations, industrial parks, highways, and shopping centers. Though agriculture is still a major economic force in the county, many new businesses have been created to employ the county's citizens. Of recent note is the growing tourism industry. With so much available to see and do, whether for a day trip or an extended vacation, it is only natural people would want to visit central Delaware. Visitors to Kent County are amazed by the many different worlds within its boundaries and will find it full of interesting sites and warm friendly people.

Like most of Delaware, the area is a wonderful mix of old and new - where the past is meshed with the present. A perfect example of this is the state capital of Dover. One can visit Legislative Hall to watch the General Assembly debating the laws of tomorrow, and then walk across The Green and stand on the site where Delaware's delegates voted to ratify the U.S. Constitution on December 7, 1787. Continue to stroll along the brick sidewalks, marvel at grand Georgian and Victorian homes, browse in specialty shops and tour the many historic state buildings. Dover is also home to several small museums including the Johnson Victrola Museum, a tribute to E. Reeves Johnson and his pioneering work in the phonograph industry; the Delaware Agricultural Museum, preserving the area's agricultural heritage; and the Biggs Museum of American Art, featuring impressive American decorative arts and furniture. Speaking of art, the Delaware Division of the Arts supports many programs in Kent County. Education in the arts is a large part of the programs, as well as support for established local artists, theater, music programs and even local festivals. As you enjoy Dover keep an eye out for the horse-drawn buggies of local Amish rolling calmly along the city streets. If you're looking for something at a bit faster pace, twice a year NASCAR racing comes to Dover International Speedway. There is also harness racing and a premiere slots/gaming facility open year-round at Dover Downs.

As impressive as the offerings of Dover are, don't forget the rest of Kent County for exciting activities. Just south of Dover one can visit the Air Mobility Command Museum at Dover Air Force Base. There you will see several types of military aircraft and can tour a C-5A Galaxy, the largest cargo plane in the free world (definitely a "you have to see it to believe it" kind of a thing). Nearby, but a world apart, is the John Dickinson Plantation. Here visitors can take a step back to 18th century Delaware at the home of the man known as the "Penman of the American Revolution." At the far south of the county is Harrington, site of the annual Delaware State Fair. It is also home to Midway Slots and Simulcast where one can enjoy more gaming and harness racing excitement. Quaint towns like Smyrna and Leipsic, and waterside communities like Bowers Beach are also a part of Kent County. Near Smyrna is the 15,978 acre Bombay Hook National Wildlife Refuge - a haven for thousands of birds and waterfowl and an important link in the Eastern flyway route for many migratory birds.

In short, Kent County is rich in its history, its people and its contemporary development. With so much to choose from, perhaps the best thing Kent County offers to residents and visitors is just that - choices. A seemingly endless list of choices for work, play and lifestyle awaits you in Kent County.

DELAWARE STATE FAIR, HARRINGTON

DELAWARE STATE FAIR, HARRINGTON

MODERN FARM OUTSIDE OF DOVER

DELAWARE STATE FAIR, HARRINGTON

Kent County is also the home to numerous farms, both large and small. Each year most of the agricultural community meets at the Delaware State Fair in Harrington. Activities at the fair continue nonstop for a week and include everything from livestock judging to rides and amusements for kids of all ages.

BOMBAY HOOK WILDLIFE REFUGE

DOCKS AT BOWERS BEACH

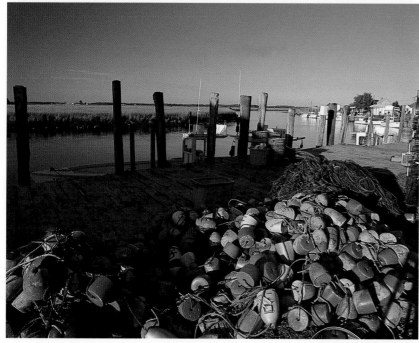
LEIPSIC FISHING DOCK

FISHING BOATS - PORT MAHON

The coast of Kent County along the Delaware River and Bay is an undiscovered treasure. There you will find Bombay Hook Wildlife Refuge which is a huge natural preservation area along the bay which attracts numerous naturalists and bird watchers. There are also small fishing towns such as Leipsic, Port Mahon and Bowers Beach which are still quiet little areas unspoiled by the rush and commercialism found along most of the east coast.

DELAWARE SEASHORE STATE PARK

THE ZWAANENDAEL MUSEUM, LEWES

CAPE MAY-LEWES FERRY

DELAWARE SEASHORE STATE PARK

Sussex County is the southern-most county and is renowned for the beautiful seashore beaches along its eastern boundary. The Cape May-Lewes Ferry operates year round, crossing the Delaware Bay several times a day, providing an important transportation link for the East Coast. In Lewes you can explore such wonders as the Zwaanendael Museum or nearby Cape Henlopen State Park.

DELAWARE TODAY
SUSSEX COUNTY

Sussex County today is a unique mix of past, present and future. Many places give up their past for the sake of progress. Sussex County has not only held onto its heritage but proudly celebrates it while maintaining a proactive platform of growth, both culturally and economically. Most people unfamiliar with Sussex County, and Delaware in general, are amazed at how much there is to see and do in its relatively small area. As the saying goes, "Good things come in small packages!" Just about any interest or pursuit - history, sports, antiques, theater and art, outdoor recreation, shopping and more - can be found in Delaware's southernmost county.

The history of Sussex County is rich and diverse. The site of the first European settlement in Delaware, the county has continued to grow and evolve in the intervening centuries. Like the Native Americans before them, these early European settlers utilized the area's abundant forests and rich soil to support themselves and their families. The many waterways, which characterize the geography of the county, were harnessed to power mills to grind grain and saw timber. The clearing of land and resulting expansion of agricultural production led to the growing exportation of the products of field and forest. A flourishing shipbuilding industry evolved, first to support the local export trade, and later to support the nation's growing maritime industry in the 19th century. With the coming of the railroad, towns began to grow, and the county's economy became more diverse. Though the economic life of Sussex County today includes a mixture of small businesses, light industry, and a growing tourism trade, agriculture has continued to play a major role. This is particularly the case with the poultry industry. Considered the birthplace of the modern broiler chicken industry, Sussex is the largest poultry-producing county in the nation.

The increasing growth of the county's economy has made Sussex an even more desirable place to work and live. The hospitable environment is being discovered by families, businesses and vacationers alike. People looking to relocate are finding southern Delaware to be an ideal place. It offers the best of both worlds, a pleasant rural feeling with cosmopolitan amenities. For those with children, the county education system is highly regarded with eight public school districts, a number of private schools and four colleges serving the county. In addition, there are technical and vocational schools (high school and college level), adult education services and corporate training facilities.

The incentives to operate one's business in Delaware are well known. In response to the needs of larger businesses, a number of industrial parks have been established in recent years. This allows corporations room to operate and grow with convenient access to transportation and other services, while maintaining the small town feel of the county. With the new growth, entrepreneurial opportunities are ever increasing and programs are available in Sussex County to assist the smallest venture to the largest corporation. Supporting many of these businesses are the large number of vacationers and visitors who have discovered the wonders of Sussex County.

The beach resorts of Rehoboth, Bethany, Dewey and Fenwick Island are well-known destinations, and deservedly so. From Slaughter Beach in the north, to Fenwick Island in the south, there are over twenty-five miles of enjoyable bay and ocean coastline. Each area offers a slightly different flavor with different attractions, such as a historic lighthouse, a boardwalk and amusement parks, arts and crafts shows, wildlife viewing and watersports. An ongoing conservation program supported by Sussex County and the state will insure that the beaches remain pristine and available for the enjoyment of both residents and visitors.

In addition to its coastline, the county has much more to offer visitors. One of Sussex County's five state parks not on the coast is Trap Pond State Park. Here one can enjoy amazing wildlife, bald cypress trees and abundant wildflowers while camping, hiking, fishing and swimming. A popular excursion is the Cape May-Lewes Ferry. Leaving from Lewes, the ferry will transport you (and your vehicle if you like) to Cape May, New Jersey for a day of exploring the historic Victorian town. Sussex County has plenty of history of its own. The towns of Bethel, Laurel, Milton, Georgetown and Lewes have continued to maintain the charm of yesteryear. Many vacationers are seeking these quaint towns for their variety of activities and small-town life. Each has some type of museum depicting local and area history and one can wander quiet streets searching antique shops for a special bargain. In Lewes, the sports-minded can charter a deep sea fishing adventure, jump on a headboat for some inshore angling or take a short drive to one of the county's many public golf courses. The Ross Plantation in Seaford is a great destination, or for a really lively day, attend the Nanticoke Indian PowWow near Millsboro each September.

To say the least there is plenty to see, do and just plain like about Sussex County. Much has changed over the years. The explorers are now tourists, and the natives are called Delawareans. But, the reasons they visit and the reasons they live here remain the same - the beauty, splendor and opportunity that is offered them in this place called Sussex County, Delaware.

LEWES HOUSE

REHOBOTH

BETHANY BEACH

CAPE HENLOPEN

The wonders of Sussex are split among great seashore towns such as Rehoboth, Lewes and Bethany Beach, and the central and western part of the county which consists of mostly quiet rural areas. Each of these beach towns offers the visitor something unique and different. The western and central part of the county is full of historic communities and scenic countryside. These towns offer numerous attractions which can be explored if you make the time.

MILFORD HOUSE

MILTON AREA FARM

SEAFORD AREA FARM

GEORGETOWN HOUSE

In quiet Sussex County communities, such as Milford, Milton and Laurel, one can stay in a cozy bed and breakfast, while shopping for antiques and enjoying the gentle pace of small-town life. Georgetown is the county-seat, and the location of many historic homes and government buildings.

QUESTIONS

To assist you with your appreciation of the information on these historic roadside markers, we have put together a series of questions. This is a "win-win" quiz because we have given you the marker number and page number where the answers can be found. We hope you find the answers both interesting and informative.

1. Where did the only battle of the Revolutionary War occur in Delaware?
    Answer: Marker 2, page 21 and marker 7, page 23

2. Who was Antoni Swart?
    Answer: Marker 3, page 21

3. What is "The Wren Nest?"
    Answer: Marker 26, page 29

4. What Delaware town was originally called Appoquinimi?
    Answer: Marker 50, page 39 and marker 74, page 47

5. Who was the only Delaware governor known to be born in a foreign country?
    Answer: Marker 54, page 41

6. What Delaware city has gone by the names of Tamakonch, Fort Casimir, Fort Trefaldigheets, and New Amstel?
    Answer: Marker 70, page 45

7. Odessa is named for what foreign city?
    Answer: Marker 74, page 47

8. What happened at "The Rocks?"
    Answer: Marker 90, page 53 and marker 39, page 35.

9. Whom did Samuel Davies term "that heroic youth?"
    Answer: Marker 93, page 53

10. What is "The Wedge?"
    Answer: Marker 112, page 59

11. Which signers of the Declaration of Independence lived in New Castle?
    Answer: Marker 70, page 45

12. What school was built on land donated by John Dickinson, the "Penman of the American Revolution?"
    Answer: Marker 22, page 29

13. When was the first Bank of Delaware organized?
    Answer: Marker 28, page 31

14. When did the du Ponts build their first powder mill in America?
    Answer: Marker 31, page 31

15. How high above sea level is the highest natural elevation in Delaware?
    Answer: Marker 34, page 33

16. What is William Julius "Judy" Johnson noted for?
    Answer: Marker 48, page 39

17. Thomas Garrett was called "Stationmaster" for what railroad?
    Answer: Marker 104, page 57

18. Who was the first Bishop of the African Methodist Episcopal Church?
    Answer: Marker 4, page 63

19. What does "kill" mean in Dutch?
    Answer: Marker 38, page 77

20. What African Methodist Episcopal Church was associated with the Underground Railroad?
    Answer: Marker 46, page 81

21. Who ordered Dover to be laid out as a town?
    Answer: Marker 17, page 69

22. When did Delaware become the first state to ratify the U.S. Constitution?
    Answer: Marker 2, page 63

23. What judge was one of the prime movers to bring the railroad to southern Delaware?
    Answer: Marker 24, page 71

24. During the Revolutionary War, whose picture was painted on the sign of King George's Tavern?
Answer: Marker 42, page 79

25. In Delaware, where is the site of one of the earliest Methodist churches in America?
Answer: Marker 48, page 81

26. When did passenger rail service end in Felton, Delaware?
Answer: Marker 49, page 83

27. In Kent County, where were German prisoners housed during World War II?
Answer: Marker 16, page 67

28. Where was the first American Legion Ambulance Service initiated?
Answer: Marker 20, page 69

29. When was rural free delivery of mail in Delaware initiated?
Answer: Marker 21, page 71

30. Who was the first African-American to be ordained an Episcopal priest?
Answer: Marker 2, page 85

31. Where was the first community college in the State of Delaware?
Answer: Marker 24, page 93

32. What did the citizens of France give the State of Delaware after WW II?
Answer: Marker 27, page 95

33. Which Union General, was Commander of Cavalry, Army of Shenandoah?
Answer: Marker 29, page 97

34. Who was the famous Civil War newspaper correspondent, journalist and author of the *Entailed Hat*?
Answer: Marker 30, page 97

35. What is the Highball Signal?
Answer: Marker 43, page 103

36. What is Return Day?
Answer: Marker 80, page 119

37. What is the Transpeninsular Line?
Answer: Marker 96, page 125.

38. Who was the first African-American President of Delaware State College?
Answer: Marker 100, page 129

39. In what year was the last ship launched at the Bethel Shipyard?
Answer: Marker 10, page 89

40. What city was originally established as "a permanent camp meeting ground and Christian seaside resort?"
Answer: Marker 19, page 93

41. In Sussex County, where were German prisoners housed during World War II?
Answer: Marker 26, page 95

42. What town was originally named Washington?
Answer: Marker 39, page 101

43. In 1876, what service was responsible for rendering aid to ships in distress or wrecked upon the sandy shoals of the Delaware Coast?
Answer: Marker 46, page 103

44. What town was originally part of a tract of land known as "Batchelor's Delight?"
Answer: Marker 49, page 105

45. Where was the first Dutch settlement on Delaware soil?
Answer: Marker 54, page 107

46. What is a Biblical name meaning space or places?
Answer: Marker 56, page 107.

47. What is one of the oldest brick structures in Sussex County?
Answer: Marker 60, page 109.

48. When and where did the commercial broiler industry in Delaware start?
Answer: Marker 68, page 113

49. What railroad provided travelers access to the Rehoboth Resort?
Answer: Marker 78, page 117

50. When was a lottery authorized to raise funds to replace the frame structure which had served as a courthouse since 1791?
Answer: Marker 94, page 125.

DELAWARE PUBLIC ARCHIVES

ARCHIVES RESEARCH ROOM

DELAWARE PUBLIC ARCHIVES

Since its establishment in 1905, the Delaware Public Archives has continued to serve as the repository of state and local government records of permanent value. Though the role of the Archives as the keeper of Delaware's documentary heritage has remained the same, there have been many changes since the program's founding nearly a century ago. Having long outgrown its first home in the basement of Delaware's State House Annex, the Archives was relocated to the Leon deValinger, Jr. Hall of Records in 1939. Though the facility was expanded in subsequent years, the growing nature of collections and increasing public use of these valuable resources had resulted in a chronic shortage of space by the 1990s. Following a successful statewide effort by supporters of the Archives, the State of Delaware began planning for a new facility in 1995. Construction of the modern state-of-the-art facility, adjoining the Hall of Records, was completed in 2001.

Throughout the years the programs and services provided by the Delaware Public Archives have continued to grow and evolve as well. Responding to the public's increasing demand for access to Archives' resources, hours have been expanded, and citizens can now visit on Saturdays and selected weeknights. If you can't make the trip, you can hop on the information highway and visit their rapidly expanding website, which has become one of the busiest in state government. Enter a classroom and you'll find that Delaware's students are learning more about the state's rich heritage through the creative use of actual materials from Archives' vast collections. Travel the state's highways and you'll learn more about the fascinating history of Delaware's communities by reading one of the many new historical markers erected in recent years. While the primary mission of the Delaware Public Archives has remained unchanged since the early days of the 20th century, efforts to find new and improved ways for telling the story of Delaware and its people will continue.

To learn more about the State Historical Markers Program and other services of the Archives, visit their website at www.archives.state.de.us, or write to: Delaware Public Archives, 121 Duke of York Street, Dover, DE 19901.

JOE A. SWISHER is retired from a career with the Federal Government and lives in Maryland. One of his goals in retirement was to pursue his interest in history. As a long time resident of Maryland, his first project was to document that state's historical markers. His many summer family vacations to the Delaware Atlantic Ocean beaches prompted this book on Delaware. His work brings to life the richness and excitement of Delaware history, along with the richness of Delaware today.

ROGER MILLER has worked as a commercial photographer for the last 27 years. His work has taken him around the world over 18 times. The Delaware historic marker book is his 22nd book. In addition to the Delaware book, he has just finished a book on the United States Naval Academy in Annapolis. He is currently working on a book on the United States Coast Guard Academy in New London, Connecticut as well as a book on America's tall ship, the USCG Barque Eagle. He lives and works in a restored 1860 house in the Union Square neighborhood of Baltimore.

This photograph is of the **DICKINSON PLANTATION**, near Dover
Back cover photograph is of **NEMOURS MANSION**, in Wilmington